# Differentiated Activities & Assessments Using the Common Core Standards

Carolyn Coil

CLC0488
ISBN 978-1-937113-05-6
www.piecesoflearning.com
Printed by McNaughton & Gunn, Inc.
Saline MI USA
04/2012

## Acknowledgements

Thank you to:

- Jolene Kercher and Kim Schmidt who read over the math units and made suggestions for improvements.
- Kathy and Stan Balsamo for their continual help in editing and layout.
- Emily Melvin who correlated the listing of Common Core Standards.
- Mona Livermont for help with layout, criteria cards, charts, and many other details.

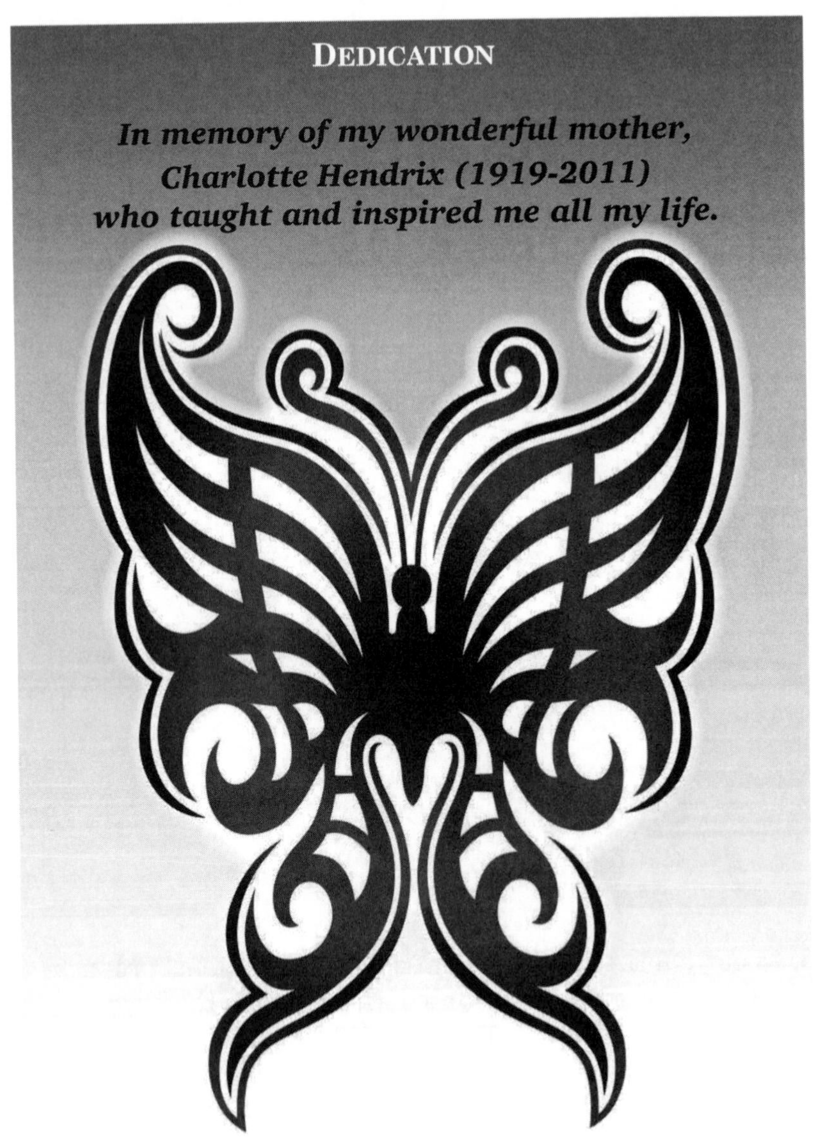
DEDICATION
*In memory of my wonderful mother,*
*Charlotte Hendrix (1919-2011)*
*who taught and inspired me all my life.*

# Table of Contents

# Introduction

## Common Core State Standards (CCSS)

The Common Core Standards (also known as the Common Core State Standards or CCSS) are the result of an initiative begun by the states and coordinated by the National Governors Association Center for Best Practices (NGA Center) and the Council of Chief State School Officers (CCSSO).

These K-12 standards in English Language Arts, Mathematics, and Literacy in History/Social Studies, Science and Technical Subjects were developed and reviewed by teachers, professional organizations, content experts, civil rights groups, postsecondary educators, administrators, and other educational experts with the goal of defining "the knowledge and skills students should have within their K-12 education careers so they graduate high school able to succeed in entry-level, credit-bearing academic college courses and workforce training programs." The CCSS provide an understandable and coherent framework for educating American children.

The Common Core State Standards are based on the most effective standards from states throughout the country and from other countries around the world. They provide guidelines about what students throughout the United States are expected to know and be able to do as a result of their schooling. The major advantage of such standards is that they are consistent for all students no matter where they live. In an age of globalization, and when many students are highly mobile and move from one state to another, such standards are essential.

According to the NGA Center and the CCSSO, these standards:

- are aligned with college and work expectations;
- are clear, understandable, and consistent;
- include rigorous content and application of knowledge through high-order skills;
- build upon the strengths and the lessons of current state standards;
- are informed by other top performing countries;
- are internationally benchmarked to prepare students to function in a global economy;
- are a living work that will be revised on a set review cycle;
- have technology blended into all strands and domains;
- focus on research as an important skill throughout all strands; and
- are evidence-based and research-based.

These standards establish appropriate benchmarks for all students and provide a common framework to guide each state in helping all students succeed. While these standards do not specify or stipulate specific texts, they do require certain critical content for all students.

They establish what students at each grade level need to learn but in general do not dictate the specific topics teachers should teach or how they should deliver instruction.

The Common Core State Standards do not specify how the states will implement and use the standards. Each state will follow its own procedures in adopting and putting them into practice. States that adopt the CCSS must use all of them but can also add up to 15% of additional content that is state-specific. As of this writing, it appears that some states are using the additional 15% while others are only using the CCSS and nothing more.

A significant advantage in using the Common Core State Standards is that they are more general with broader curriculum application and can potentially lead to higher-level thinking and mastery of 21st century skills rather than focus on lower-level test-prep answers. Overall there is an increased level of rigor expected when using the CCSS.

The Common Core State Standards focus on English Language Arts (ELA) and Mathematics. Many of the ELA standards balance the reading of literature with the reading of informational texts. The expectation is for an integrated model of literacy so that these are not taught in isolation. The Mathematics standards feature an internationally benchmarked integrated model of math instruction, particularly at the high school level.

Additionally, because the 6-12 Language Arts standards also focus on literacy standards in social studies, science, and technical subjects, these standards provide us with wide latitude in both content and in ways to teach. Instead of focusing on specific content mastery the Common Core Standards rely on major concepts, ideas, and skills that direct students to use the content to examine questions, to look at multiple issues, and to find a variety of ways to solve problems.

Because the elements discussed above have often been the focus of curriculum and instruction for gifted students, educators are able to use and extend the Common Core State Standards to enhance the learning of these students.

## English Language Arts (ELA) Standards

The College and Career Readiness (CCR) Anchor Standards provide a general outline of, and provide the framework for, the English Language Arts standards. These anchor standards are the same across all grade levels, and the grade-level standards originate from them. The grade-level standards are more specific but in each case relate to one of the anchor standards.

The English Language Arts standards are organized in strands. The four strands are:

- reading,
- writing,
- speaking and listening, and
- language.

The ELA standards highlight two different kinds of vocabulary — domain-specific and general academic. The domain-specific vocabulary focuses on words that are used in a certain subject area such as science vocabulary or history vocabulary. The general academic vocabulary includes words of increasing difficulty that can be used throughout the curriculum in any subject area.

## Mathematics Standards

The CCSS for Mathematics have two types of standards:

1. Standards for Mathematical Practice – These are the same across grade levels and describe varieties of mathematical expertise that students need to develop at all grade levels. These include:

    - make sense of problems and persevere in solving them;
    - reason abstractly and quantitatively;
    - construct viable arguments and critique the reasoning of others;
    - model with mathematics;
    - use appropriate tools strategically;
    - attend to precision;
    - look for and make use of structure; and
    - look for and express regularity in repeated reasoning.

2. Standards for Mathematical Content – These standards balance procedure and understanding. They are grade-specific standards that sequentially build a student's understanding of how to think and work mathematically.

The Mathematics standards referenced in the units in this book are from the Standards for Mathematical Content. However, while not specifically listed, many of them include the Standards for Mathematical Practice.

## DIFFERENTIATION: WHAT IS IT?

Simply stated, differentiated instruction allows each student to learn at the depth, complexity, and pace that is most beneficial to him or her. Differentiating curriculum and instruction is a rich and effective approach to use when providing for the needs of all students, including those with special educational needs such as students with learning disabilities, gifted and talented students, and English language learners.

Differentiation is required as educators work with diverse groups of students while using the same set of Common Core State Standards. They have to be modified for some students and extended or expanded for others. The amount and difficulty of both general academic vocabulary and domain-specific vocabulary has to be taken into account when working with English language learners or special education students. They need ways to challenge our brightest students. Differentiation is the structuring mechanism to use so that our daily classroom instruction can do all of these things.

**The philosophy of differentiation includes structuring classrooms so that there are provisions for:**

1. **Different ways to take in, work with, and learn information and different ways for students to show what they know.** *This can include basing student activities on multiple intelligences, learning modalities, learning styles, or learning preferences. It generally means giving students choices in project- problem- and product-based learning.*

2. **Differing amounts of time to complete the work.** *Educators know that even when you give every student exactly the same work, every student does not complete the work at exactly the same time. Differentiation allows for differences in pacing and removes us from the "factory model" of education.*

3. **Different approaches due to language acquisition and cultural differences.** *Students not only come to us knowing different languages as their first language, but they also come with different amounts of exposure to language and skill in using it. They come from cultures that may have very different messages about education, ranging from "school is the most important thing you do" to "why bother to even go to school anyway?"*

4. **Different levels of thinking, readiness, skills, and/or ability.** *Students in a given classroom are never all on exactly the same level. This is true even in a theoretically homogeneous classroom! Some start well below grade level, while others may have mastered most of the grade-level work. Because of this, it is foolish for our classroom or school goal to be to move everyone onto grade level. This is impossible for some students and, if this is the only goal, other students might as well go home for the year! Differentiation takes every student from their starting point and helps them make progress as they learn new things.*

5. **Different assignments for students in the same classroom.** *A differentiated classroom includes students who are working on a variety of different assignments. Usually these activities are centered around the same theme or topic and/or standards, but the activities various students are doing are based on what they need, not on what everyone else is doing.*

6. **Different means to assess what has been learned.** *Assessment seems to be the most difficult aspect of differentiation for many teachers. This may be because differentiated curriculum and instruction calls for differentiated assessments, yet many assessments that schools focus on are standardized assessments. Rather than trying to combine them, it is more valuable to delineate what type of assessment is being used at a given time. For the foreseeable future, educators will probably use both. Use the chart below to decide which type of assessment you are (or should be) using at a given time.*

### COMPARING TYPES OF ASSESSMENT

| Standardized Assessment | Differentiated Assessment |
|---|---|
| • Based on everyone meeting the grade-level standard | • Based on each student making individual progress |
| • Compares one student to a group of students at the same age or grade | • Compares one student to himself or herself over time |
| • Testing and traditional report cards | • Differentiated projects, rubrics, and non-traditional report cards |
| • Mostly summative assessment | • Mostly pre-assessment and formative assessment |

***Differentiation transforms students from caterpillars . . . into butterflies***

The assessments in this book are differentiated assessments. Using differentiated assessments leads to greater success and achievement on high-stakes standardized tests.

# Coil Horizontal and Vertical Differentiation Model™

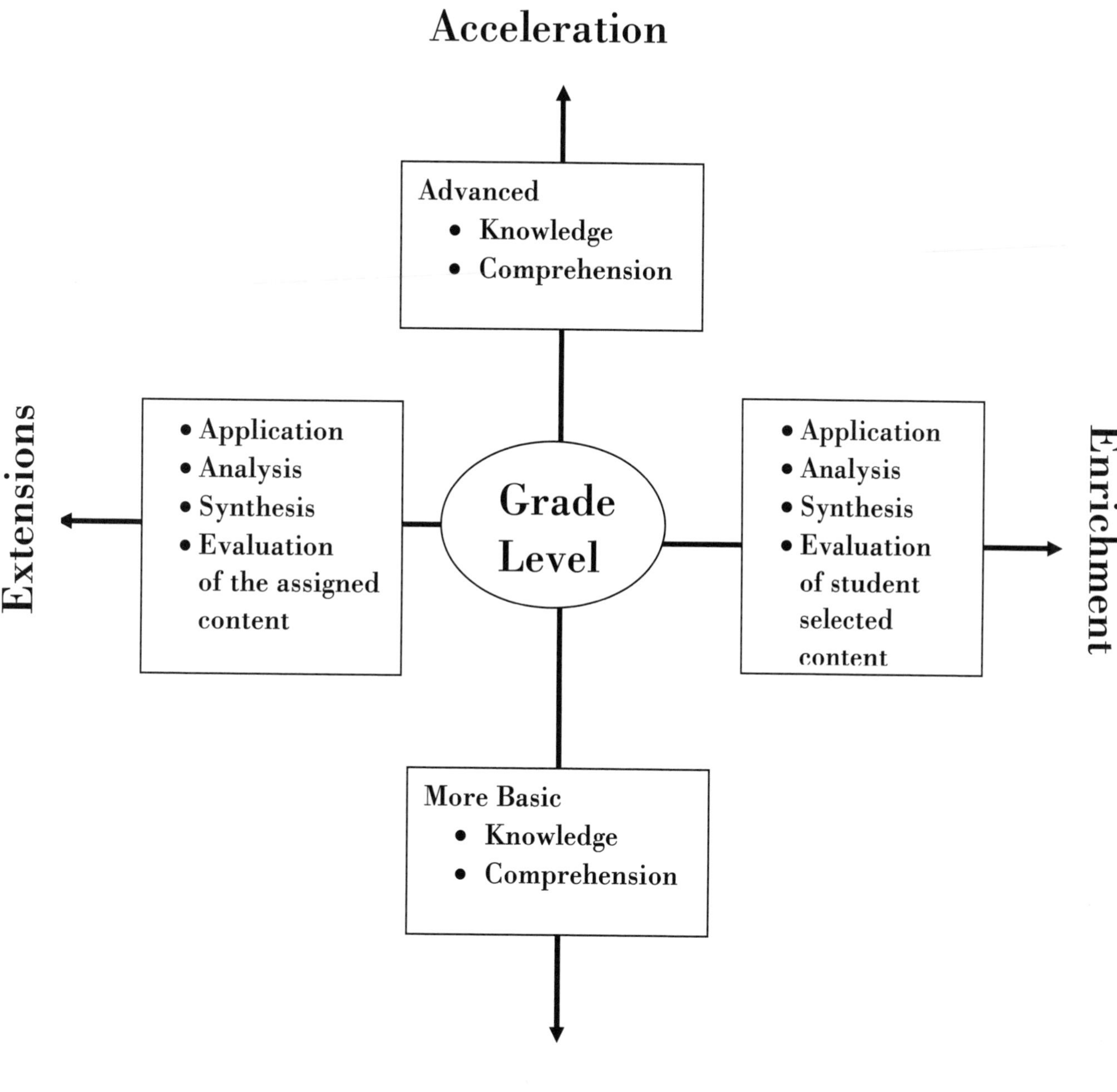

## THE COIL HORIZONTAL AND VERTICAL DIFFERENTIATION MODEL™

We can look at differentiation both vertically and horizontally. Most students, teachers, and parents have traditionally looked at learning in the vertical mode. This is where our content scope and sequence resides, and many state standards in the past have focused on covering the vertical content.

On the vertical axis, "Grade Level" is in the middle. Generally, if a student is functioning below grade level, we work to bring that student up, using various types of remediation and intervention strategies. Indeed, this is one type of differentiation and is necessary when teaching sequential skills.

**Remediation** means that students have holes or gaps in their knowledge, skills, or learning that need to be patched before they can move on to the next skill level. The assumption that all students begin the school year at the same starting point is faulty. Many times students lack the required skills and knowledge to do the work their grade level requires. Determining exactly what needs to be remediated for an individual student or for groups of students and then having a plan to achieve is essential for student success in today's schools.

On the top of the vertical axis is acceleration. In general, when parents complain that their son or daughter already knows the work and is bored in your class, what they probably think they want for their child is for you to progress vertically more quickly through the curriculum.

**Acceleration** allows students to study the material at a faster pace and/or at a higher grade level than would normally be the case. Collaborating with another teacher at a higher grade level is one way to gather information and resources to use in acceleration. The difficulty with using this approach is that it requires vertical planning among teachers at different grade levels, something that can be a challenge to schedule and to implement.

The greatest problem in merely using the vertical approach is that this approach generally includes only the two lower levels of thinking, Knowledge and Comprehension. Most of the higher levels of thinking now required by the Common Core State Standards are lost if differentiation remains solely in the vertical mode.

The horizontal axis illustrates the other approaches to use in a differentiated classroom when teaching the Common Core State Standards. The horizontal approach generally incorporates the higher levels of thinking: Application, Analysis, Synthesis, and Evaluation. The two horizontal approaches are Enrichment and Extensions.

**Enrichment** activities focus on studying areas or topics that are not included in the regular curriculum. These activities broaden students' knowledge and understanding about a wide range of subjects. Through exposure to enrichment activities, students may develop areas of interest about which they previously knew little. Enrichment also allows students to explore current areas of interest in greater depth. This can lead to opportunities for investigations of real problems with links to the world outside of school.

**Extensions** use the regular curriculum as a starting point and allow students to delve into a subject more deeply or look at aspects of the subject or unit of study that may not otherwise be considered. Extensions work particularly well with students who already know the basics or who complete the regular assignments quickly and need additional challenges for their learning.

Many of the reading and writing Common Core State Standards focus on developing research skills, using digital media, using informational texts, and drawing evidence to support analysis, reflection, and research. They and many similar Common Core State Standards require that all students function on the horizontal as well as the vertical axis of the model.

Pictured are two arcs for differentiated learning. Struggling students will need remediation. Advanced students will need acceleration. Some students may need both. Yet when using the CCSS, all students will need instruction in the horizontal mode as well so that all will be exposed to the higher levels of thinking.

**Patterns for Differentiated Learning**

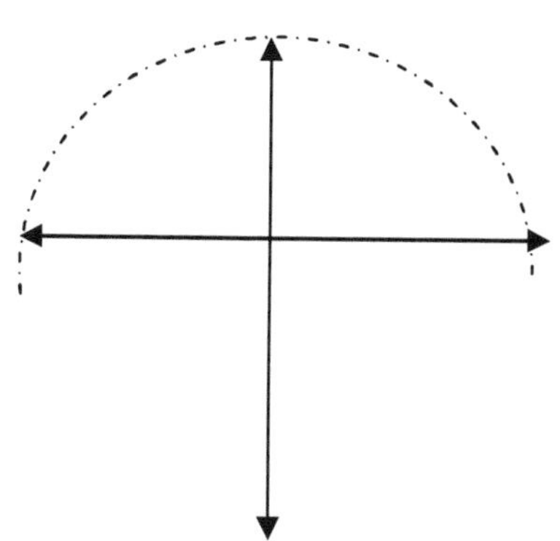

**Advanced Learners**

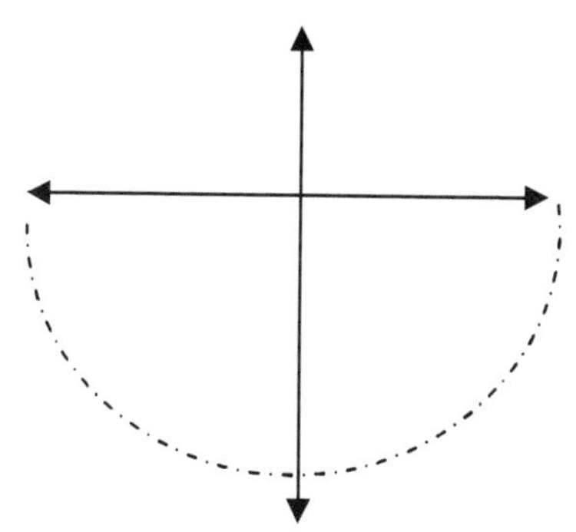

**Struggling Students**

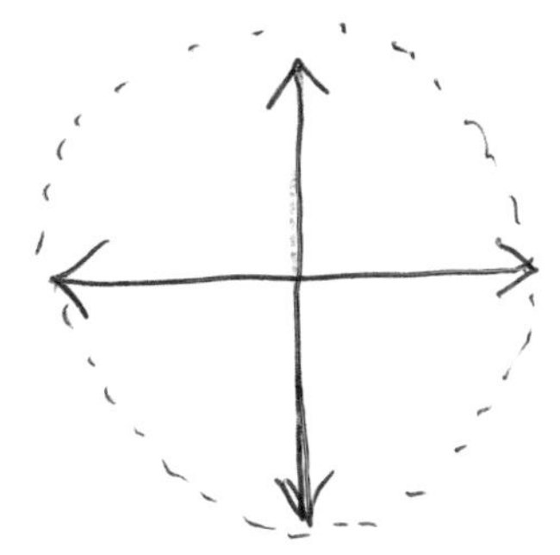

Dual Label

## Differentiated Activities and Assessments

The Common Core State Standards need to be differentiated for gifted, special education, ELL students, and other students with special needs. These standards incorporate only the essentials, thus they need to be modified and supplemented for special groups of students. One of the purposes of this book is to show how these standards can be used with differentiated curriculum, instruction, and assessment.

The Common Core State Standards require a depth of learning that is best reflected through performance tasks, projects, product differentiation, creative and critical thinking activities, and the development of research skills. The activities and assessments in this book are designed as examples of how the CCSS can be implemented in the classroom. In each lesson or unit, the Anchor Standard is indicated, and some (but not all) of the Common Core State Standards being addressed. In some cases, also included are specific content objectives.

The challenge in writing this book is that most of my activities and assessments cover a multitude of standards. That is, however, a goal of developing frameworks for the CCSS. Combining standards as curriculum and activities are designed connects learning. In writing these units, a number of the Common Core Standards are addressed in each unit. Because of this, I have taken the liberty to accentuate just some of the standards in each lesson or unit plan. You will then be able to use the standards high-lighted as well as find other standards that you can emphasize during your instruction.

Many of the activities in this book are student choice activities. When one or two of the student choice activities focus on a particular Common Core State Standard, this standard is included within the assessment of the individual choice activity. For example, there are several standards that deal with oral presentation skills. If a student choice activity includes an oral presentation, this standard is incorporated in the assessment of that particular activity.

## HOW TO USE THIS BOOK

Following the Introduction and Criteria Cards sections, this book is divided into sections based on the type of differentiation strategy used. At the beginning of each of these sections is an introduction to the strategy and description of how it is implemented. Next is a list of the units or lessons using the particular strategy. Each of these incorporates some of the Common Core State Standards. At the end of each section are blank forms so that you can write your own lessons and units.

Each section contains units with activities and assessments at various grade levels. Many of these sample units can be adapted at several different grade levels. Try those that best fit your class and grade level. After you have tried several, you may want to look at others you can adapt.

The CD includes reproducible pages with all of the units in WORD format. This means you can customize the wording. You might want to change the content or topic, add or delete a specific standard, or change something in the assessment of the activities.

The types of unit or lesson formats in this book include:

- Curriculum Compacting,
- Individual Lesson Plan (ILP)™,
- Primary ILP™,
- Questivities™,
- Tic-Tac-Toe, and
- Tiered Lessons & Units.

# Index by Subjects

# CRITERIA CARDS

## Criteria Cards: What Are They and How Do I Use Them?

Frequently you may have the same generic criteria for certain products, projects, processes or performances regardless of the specific academic content they cover. These are most likely processes you want the student to focus on at all times or products they do more than once. These may well be products and processes they do for several different teachers. A number of the Common Core State Standards such as drawing evidence from texts or steps to math problem solving lend themselves to generic criteria.

Other generic processes include certain writing conventions (grammar, mechanics and sentence structure) or a skill like research skills or organizational skills. It may be classroom expectations such as turning in one's work on time. In addition, there are hundreds of products and projects students can do. Occasionally these cards will focus on a process done in a certain subject over and over again such as editing or doing a science lab report.

A great assessment short cut and time saver is to assess these products and processes by using Criteria Cards that students can draw on and refer to over and over again. These cards have short, easily understood lists of criteria (generally 4-6) that students can look at each time they use the same process or complete the same product or project. If all teachers at a given grade level in elementary school or throughout a team or department at the middle and high school level would use the same criteria cards, students benefit greatly.

In addition, if we start articulating and giving a scope and sequence to student products and performances in the same way we do curriculum content, teachers at one grade level could pass along criteria cards to teachers at the next grade level. Wouldn't it be nice to know that all of the third graders who come to you on the first day of 4$^{th}$ grade have had experience making a brochure or creating a PowerPoint or developing a Venn diagram or designing a diorama? We rarely have such information, however, so we make assumptions about what our students know how to do. Many times we really don't know what their experience is. Criteria cards at different grade levels could definitely help with this dilemma!

On page 23 is a form to use with the other teachers at your school to establish a scope and sequence of products and performances. Creating this scope and sequence is similar to the process of curriculum mapping except that the focus is merely on the products and performances, not the content. Meet in grade level groups first and then share with the teachers the grade below you and the grade above you. This will be helpful in learning what your students already know how to do and to what projects or products they need to be introduced.

Criteria cards are used in the assessments throughout this book. Some are used only once, but many are used several times. On pages 18 – 21 are criteria cards for 40 products. Additionally, on pages 25 – 30 you will find six full-page criteria cards to use with primary students.

These criteria cards cover all of the criteria cards referred to in the assessments of units throughout this book. They are a beginning point for developing many more of your own.

## Criteria Cards for Older Students

- ABC Book
- Blog
- Brochure
- Business Letter
- Cartoon
- Chart
- Collage
- Comic Book/Comic Strip
- Crossword Puzzle
- Debate
- Diagram
- Diorama
- Drawing
- Flip Book
- Flowchart
- Game
- Information Cube
- Interview
- Journal
- Map
- Mobile
- Model
- Monologue
- Montage
- Mosaic
- Oral Presentation/Report
- Picture Book
- Picture Postcard
- Podcast
- Poem
- Pop-up Book
- Poster
- PowerPoint Presentation
- Radio Report
- Scrapbook
- Slide Show
- Skit
- Song
- Time Line
- Venn Diagram

These Criteria Cards are on pages 18-21.

# Product Criteria Cards

| ABC Book | Chart |
|---|---|
| 1. Focuses on one topic or idea<br>2. Has at least one word and picture about the idea from every letter of the alphabet<br>3. One page per letter<br>4. Alphabetical order<br>5. Neat with correct spelling | 1. Has two or more sections divided by lines<br>2. Title and subtitles<br>3. Shows information clearly<br>4. Neat with correct spelling |
| **Blog**<br>1. Posted on a web page<br>2. Clearly stated writer's opinion on topic<br>3. Has supporting evidence and facts<br>4. Includes link to resources, pictures, or video<br>5. Correct grammar and spelling<br>6. Allows for comments from others | **Collage**<br>1. Has a solid backing<br>2. Pictures/objects overlap<br>3. Title/labels spelled correctly<br>4. Visually attractive and neat<br>5. Pictures/objects relate to topic |
| **Brochure**<br>1. Pictures relate to topic<br>2. Attractive and neat layout<br>3. Folded with information on each panel<br>4. Neat and clear writing highlighting important points<br>5. Correct spelling | **Comic Book/Comic Strip**<br>1. Frames in correct sequence<br>2. Tells story or idea through pictures<br>3. Characters/objects clearly drawn<br>4. Clear writing with correct spelling<br>5. Humor<br>6. Original and creative |
| **Business Letter**<br>1. Heading – your name, address and date<br>2. Inside address – recipient's name and address<br>3. Salutation<br>4. Body – main part of the letter<br>5. Closing and signature | **Crossword Puzzle**<br>1. Each word intersects with another in at least one space<br>2. Correct spelling<br>3. Accurate definitions indicating across and down<br>4. Neatly and clearly done |
| **Cartoon**<br>1. Conveys a message<br>2. Clear writing with correct spelling<br>3. Neatly drawn<br>4. Humorous<br>5. Creative and original | **Debate**<br>1. Observes allotted time<br>2. States opinion clearly<br>3. Backs up opinion with evidence from reliable sources<br>4. Respectful of other side; no name calling |

| | |
|---|---|
| **Diagram**<br>1. Items in logical and accurate order<br>2. Visually shows relationship between parts or ideas<br>3. Neat drawing and writing<br>4. Object or process drawn accurately | **Information Cube**<br>1. Cube is sturdy and has six sides<br>2. Has required information on each side of the cube<br>3. Accurate information<br>4. Neat and visually attractive |
| **Diorama**<br>1. Realistic depiction of scene<br>2. Sides have background scenery<br>3. 3-dimensional figures/objects in foreground<br>4. Durable construction<br>5. Accurate | **Interview**<br>1. appropriate questions<br>2. script<br>3. sequential<br>4. personal presentation communication skills |
| **Drawing**<br>1. Pictures are clear and understandable<br>2. Neatly done<br>3. Shows topic accurately | **Journal**<br>1. Has several entries (at least 5)<br>2. Tells about events that have happened<br>3. Includes reflections or opinions about the events<br>Correct spelling and grammar |
| **Flip Book**<br>1. Front page is short and subsequent pages get longer and longer<br>2. Major topic of page can be seen in a title on the bottom<br>3. When pages are turned, top and bottom address the same topic | **Map**<br>1. Correct location of places<br>2. Clearly written key and symbols<br>3. Has scale and compass rose<br>4. Labels/places spelled correctly<br>5. Shapes of places and distances are accurate Neatness |
| **Flowchart**<br>1. Has items in sequential order<br>2. Shows relationship between items by use of arrows or lines<br>3. Labels and items are neatly written<br>4. Short explanation of each item | **Mobile**<br>1. Items are balanced and hang from a central point or structure<br>2. Visually appealing<br>3. Relevant to topic<br>4. Creative use of materials<br>5. Well-constructed |
| **Game**<br>1. Clear and understandable rules<br>2. Well-constructed<br>3. Visually appealing<br>4. Relates to topic being studied | **Model**<br>1. Accurate representation<br>2. Durable and well-constructed<br>3. Neatness<br>4. Creative use of materials |

### Monologue

1. Spoken by one person
2. Explains a topic, feelings, opinion, etc.
3. Clear pronunciation
4. Voice is loud enough for all to hear
   Stays within time limits

### Montage

1. Uses pictures and/or video clips
2. Visuals done in quick succession
3. Sequence of visuals tells a story or gives information
4. May have music to go with visuals
5. Technology works correctly

### Mosaic

1. Picture or design clearly shown
2. Uses small bits of paper, glass, tile or other materials to make picture
3. Neatness
4. Has a solid backing

### Oral Presentation/Report

1. Clear speaking loud enough for all to hear
2. Good eye contact
3. Uses gestures and visuals
4. Correct timing

### Picture Book

1. Each page has words and a picture
2. Picture is clear and understandable
3. Words help explain what the picture is about

### Picture Postcard

1. Picture in color on front of card
2. Picture is clear and understandable
3. Size 4"x5" or 4"x6"
4. Space for message on back

### Podcast

1. Audio released on the Internet
2. Can be downloaded by others
3. Gives accurate information about the topic
4. Speaking is clear and understandable
5. Stays within time limits

### Poem

1. Appropriate format and poetic structure
2. Title
3. Rich vocabulary
4. Relevant to subject
   Correct spelling, mechanics and punctuation

### Pop-up Book

1. Has 3-D paper objects on some pages
2. 3-D objects pop up when the page is opened
3. 3-D objects fold into the book when the page is not open
4. Neat and colorful

### Poster

1. On poster board
2. Legible, neat writing
3. Has visuals about topic
4. Has title and labels spelled correctly
5. Neat with white space

| **PowerPoint Presentation** | **Skit** |
|---|---|
| 1. Visually appealing<br>2. Pictures and words are coordinated<br>3. Incorporates technological options<br>4. Technology works appropriately<br>5. At least 10 slides | 1. Realistic dialogue about the topic<br>2. Actions and words support plot<br>3. Script and acting are coordinated<br>4. Costumes and props help tell story<br>Voices are loud enough to be heard |
| **Radio Report** | **Song** |
| 1. Clear and understandable<br>2. Uses descriptive words<br>3. Recording quality is good<br>4. Has sound effects or music<br>Stays within time limits | 1. Appropriate content<br>2. Has a rhythm<br>3. Words and music go together<br>4. Can be sung; auditory appeal |
| **Scrapbook** | **Time Line** |
| 1. At least 10 pages<br>2. Has a variety of pictures and words on each page<br>3. Shows and explains your topic well<br>Visually attractive | 1. Title<br>2. Chronological order<br>3. Important events/dates indicated<br>4. Well-plotted time spans<br>5. Neat and legible<br>6. Correct spelling |
| **Slide Show** | **Venn Diagram** |
| 1. Has at least the minimum number of slides<br>2. Slides are in logical order<br>3. Communicates information effectively<br>4. Has audio or you give an explanation of each slide | 1. Has two or more overlapping circles<br>2. Shows similarities and differences<br>3. Has title and conclusions<br>4. Neat and clear writing<br>7. Accurate |

## Criteria Cards: Write Your Own

| | |
|---|---|
| | |
| | |
| | |
| | |

## Scope and Sequence for Products and Performances

**Grade level _______**

**For your grade level, which products/performances:**

- Are introduced for the first time?

- Which products/performances do students know but need guidance in making/doing them?

- Which products/performances should students know how to make/do independently?

## Criteria Cards for Primary Students

Criteria cards for young students must be a full page in size, easy to read and understand, and should include a picture or other visual. Sample criteria cards for primary students include:



On page 31 is a blank criteria card to use when you write your own cards.

## Using Criteria Cards: Helpful Hints K-3

- Design product criteria cards with your students as you introduce each product.
- Make the language on the cards simple enough that it is completely understandable to your students.
- Write your criteria cards on full sheets of paper.
- Include a picture of the product as well as the criteria for the product. If possible, use a digital camera, and take a picture of each student with his/her product. Then cut and paste this picture onto his/her individual criteria card.
- Post each criteria card on the wall or bulletin board for easy reference.
- You might want to color-code the cards according to categories such as Visual, Written, Hands-on, Speaking, etc. or according to the Common Core State Standards they are addressing.
- Do a scope and sequence of criteria cards for products and performances that students learn and/or master at each grade level. It is best for the primary teachers to begin this task and pass along their cards to the teachers at the next grade level.

Criteria cards for older students are generally smaller, often with 10 criteria cards on each page. Older students can carry them in their notebooks or as a document on a computer, Smart Phone, or iPAD. Criteria cards are used in assessments throughout this book.

Note: A good resource that includes a CD with 88 cards in a customizable WORD file:
*Product Criteria Cards*
by Merritt and Coil.
Pieces of Learning. www.piecesoflearning.com

# Chart

1. Has two or more sections

2. Lines divide each section

3. Neat writing

4. Title tells what it is about

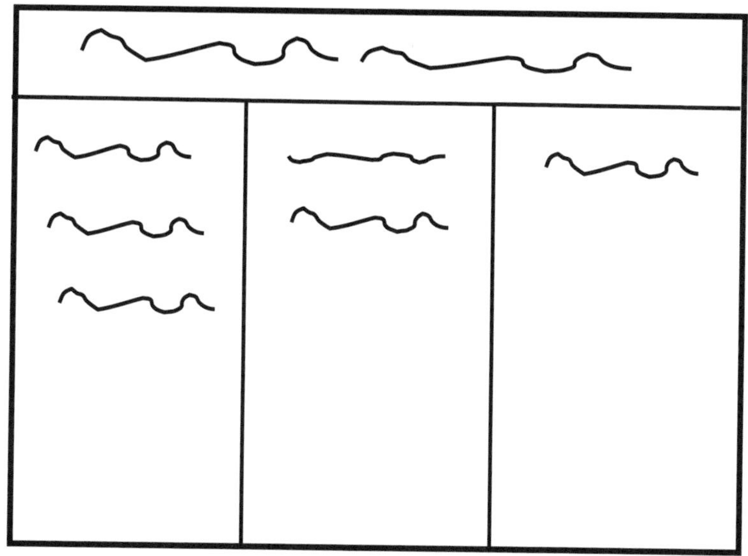

# Collage

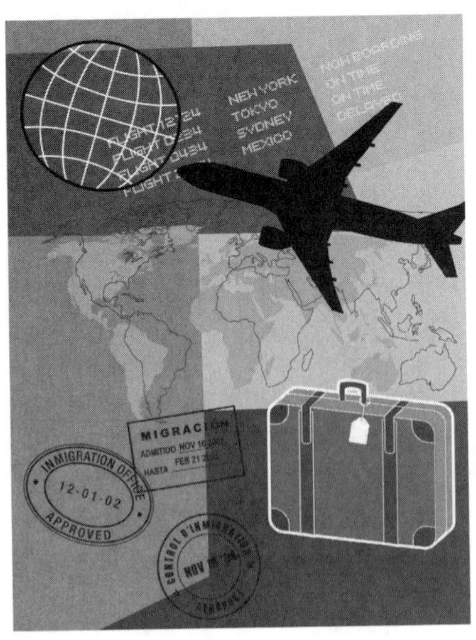


1. All pictures overlap

2. Shows examples of the topic

3. Pictures are glued on a poster board or construction paper

4. Neat

# Comic Strip

1. Has at least 3 frames

2. Tells a story

3. Has drawings

4. Shows talking through balloons with tails

# Drawing

1. Uses pencil, pen, crayons, or markers on paper or another flat object

2. Shows something you know about

3. Understandable to others

4. Neatly done

# Song

1. Has rhyming words

2. Has a tune you can sing

3. At least four lines long

4. Words and music go together

# Venn Diagram

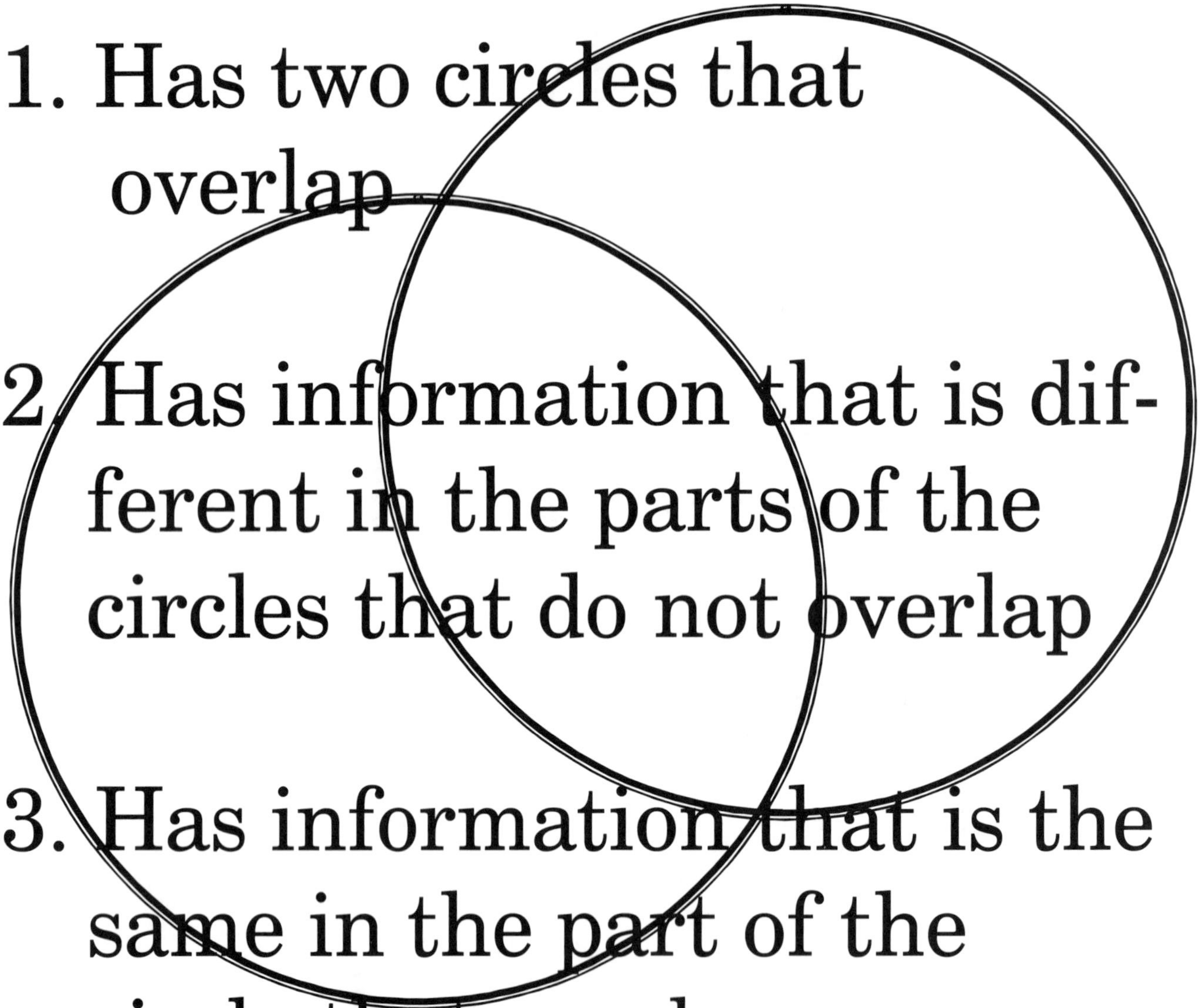

1. Has two circles that overlap

2. Has information that is different in the parts of the circles that do not overlap

3. Has information that is the same in the part of the circle that overlaps

4. Has a title

# Name of Product

1.

2.

3.

4.

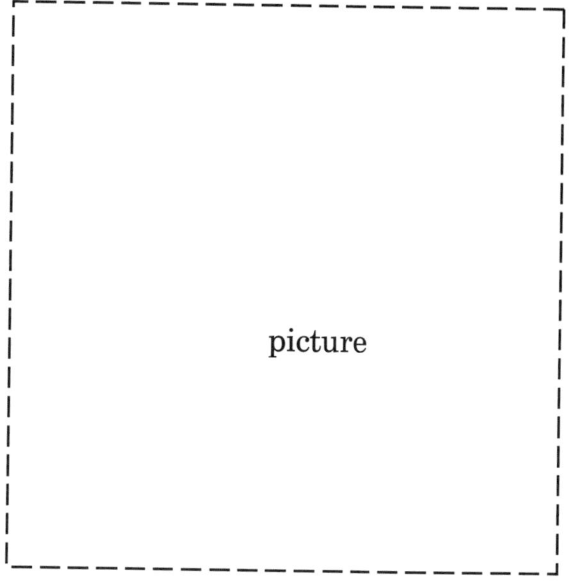

# CURRICULUM COMPACTING

## Curriculum Compacting: What Is It?

Do you have students who already know some of the skills and knowledge you will be teaching during a given week, grading period, or unit of work?

Teachers generally answer yes to that question but often do not act on that information about their students. Research suggests that high-ability elementary students know between 35-50% of the curriculum in the five major subjects (reading, language skills, math, science and social studies). Middle and high school students might know as much as 20% of the curriculum.

Curriculum Compacting is a strategy that works to challenge those who already know the material you are teaching. It extends and enriches the Common Core Standards for students who already understand the basics. Developed by Dr. Joseph Renzulli and Linda Smith at the University of Connecticut, Curriculum Compacting involves pre-testing or using some other type of pre-assessment data to find out which students have already mastered basic skills and knowledge.

For ***pre-assessment***, you can use the same final test you use at the end of the unit, or use an alternate test or set of questions. For K-2 students, teachers often use oral assessments or some type of running records that they are already using with each student. A number of teachers like the *"Most Difficult First"* strategy. They ask students to complete the most difficult problems or questions from each section of the unit, selecting those that represent specific knowledge or skills the student must know. If a student can complete those correctly, it seems evident that there is no need for him or her to do the easier problems covering the same knowledge and skills.

In some middle school and most high school courses you may want to take one or two days to introduce the unit and concepts before doing this type of pre-assessment. Some students will catch on quickly and then can move into more challenging alternate activities.

One practical way to implement Curriculum Compacting is to use a form called the *Curriculum Compactor* to document and record all modifications in curriculum.

- In the far left column, list the skills/content/knowledge students need to know. This could be for the week, the month, the unit of study, or the grading period. In general it is best to select skills and knowledge that are easy to assess in terms of mastery. Often this is the more "cut-and-dried" portions of the curriculum.
- In the center column, use the data you have collected to document the student's mastery of the items listed in the left column.
- In the far right column, indicate alternate activities the student can complete while the rest of the class is working to master the curriculum standards and required knowledge and skills.

Alternate activities are usually extensions or enrichment in the same subject area, topic and standards from which the student "bought" the time. Sometimes, however, they may be activities from different subject areas or from the student's individual interest area. Do not include more of the same kinds of worksheets, questions, and review assignments. Curriculum compacting should be used to provide the student with opportunities for higher-level thinking and advanced study.

Students who compact the curriculum should have notebooks, folders, or separate sections of their course notebooks for Compactor work. In it should be all assessments showing mastery with dates, all Compactor forms, the work from alternate activities, and some type of record keeper or feedback form to show what the student accomplished each day during Compacting time.

Note that the starting point for your compacting students is mastery of the knowledge and skills. Therefore you want to make sure that their grade reflects this mastery as well as the alternate work they are doing. Nothing destroys Curriculum Compacting more quickly than for the compacting students, because they are doing more challenging work, to regularly receive lower marks or grades than the other students who are doing regular classroom assignments.

12 examples of 3-column Curriculum Compactors for various subjects and for different ages and grades follow. Additionally, there are assessments for each of the compacting Alternate Activities. Use these with your students as appropriate and also as models when you write your own. Use the blank forms on pages 61-62 when you write your own Curriculum Compactors and Assessments.

Curriculum Compactors and Alternate Activity assessments include:



For more information about Curriculum Compacting, see <u>*Successful Teaching in the Differentiated Classroom*</u> by Carolyn Coil

## Helpful Hints for Curriculum Compacting

- The teacher sets the mastery level for the standards.
- Look at your data, and decide what data to use to establish mastery of the topic or standards.
- Give students a choice of 2-4 alternate learning activities. More is too many because students take too much learning time just trying to choose what activity to work on.
- The one choice a student never has is the choice to do nothing! Monitor your compacting students. If you see a compacting student doing nothing or doing something inappropriate with his or her time, immediately tell the student to return to the regular class instruction. Give him/her another chance to do compacting activities the next day.
- Procedures must be established concerning the wise use of compacting time. These should be clear to students before they begin compacting. These procedures could be developed and agreed upon by the whole class.
- Use compacting to teach organization and time management skills.
- Students who have compacted out of regular classroom work need to be held accountable for their learning time. Use some type of Learning Log or Student Feedback form for your compacting students.
- A student's grade should never be impacted negatively by doing more challenging work. By their very nature, Alternate Activities should be more challenging, more rigorous, and more difficult. Use the pre-test grade where the student demonstrates mastery as a baseline and give additional credit for alternate activities.
- Alternate activities are never busy work. Instead, these activities must truly extend, accelerate, or enrich the curriculum. Challenge should be the emphasis.
- Look for student activities that would be good for your compacting students. Once you are aware of this strategy, you will see such activities everywhere. Planning them well so that students can do them independently is the key to success.
- Communication with parents is important. They need to know what compacting is, how it works, and how it affects their child.

# CURRICULUM COMPACTOR
## Alphabet

**Anchor Standard: LA/Language: Conventions of Standard English**

**Common Core Standards:**

- Demonstrate command of the conventions of standard English grammar and usage when writing or speaking.
- Print all upper and lower case letters.

**Student's Name** ______________________________

| Skill/Knowledge/ Content | Documentation of Mastery | Student Choice Alternate Activities |
|---|---|---|
| Recognize all 26 letters of the alphabet in both upper and lower case. | Oral assessment – 100% correct when letters are not shown in alphabetical order | 1. Cut out pictures from magazines or newspapers, or draw pictures showing items that begin with each letter.<br>Create an ABC book with one page for each letter.<br>Paste or draw the pictures on each page.<br>Put both the upper case and lower case letter on each page.<br><br>2. Invent a dance or cheer where your body shows one letter at a time.<br>Teach it to the class saying each letter as you do it.<br>Have the class repeat each letter after you say it.<br><br>3. Become the class expert in one letter.<br>Write and draw a picture of at least 10 words beginning with this letter. |

*Note: This standard is a Common Core Anchor Standard and covers all grammar instruction K-12. Use this format with any grammar skills and give higher-level alternate activities to the students who have already mastered the skills.

# CURRICULUM COMPACTOR ASSESSMENT

## Alternate Activities
## Alphabet

Alternate Activities should be more challenging than those done by students who are learning the skills or material. You may incorporate points into this assessment or use it as feedback to the student without points. Remember, students working on Alternate Activities in a Compactor have already demonstrated mastery of the skills. Their final grade should reflect that mastery plus the work done on the Alternate Activities.

**1. ABC Book**

____Book has pictures for each letter
____Total of 26 pages, one for each letter
____Shows upper case and lower case for each letter
____Neatly done and readable

Comments:

**2. Dance or Cheer**

____Has a movement showing each letter
____Says each letter as it is performed
____Leads class in repeating the letter

*Suggested extension:*
*Have cards or other visuals for each letter that are shown during the performance.*

Comments:

**3. Letter Expert**

____Chooses one letter
____Writes at least 10 words beginning with the letter
____Has pictures illustrating each word
____Correct spelling

Comments:

# CURRICULUM COMPACTOR

## Grammar Skills – Adjectives and Adverbs

**Anchor Standard: LA/Language: Conventions of Standard English**

**Common Core Standards:**

- Demonstrate command of the conventions of standard English grammar and usage when writing or speaking.*
- Correctly use frequently confused words.

**Student's Name** ________________________________

| Skill/Knowledge/ Content | Documentation of Mastery | Student Choice Alternate Activities |
|---|---|---|
| Identify and correctly punctuate adjective and adverb clauses. | 90% correct on the pre-test | 1. Create a PowerPoint presentation with 10 slides. These slides will have 5 interesting sentences that have adjective clauses and 5 sentences that have adverb clauses.<br>Omit any needed commas (but know where they should go).<br>We will use your presentation to offer practice to the rest of the class.<br><br>2. Write and recite a humorous poem to the class about how to identify and punctuate adjective and adverb clauses. |
| Demonstrate correct usage of comparative and superlative forms of adjectives and adverbs. | 90% correct on the pre-test | 3. Create a poster explaining how and when to use the comparative and superlative forms of adjectives and adverbs.<br><br>4. Create a brochure showing the most common mistakes when using the comparative and superlative forms of adjectives and adverbs.<br>The brochure should also have reminders and hints about how not to make these mistakes. |

*Note: This standard is a Common Core Anchor Standard and covers all grammar instruction K-12. Use this format with any grammar skills and give higher-level alternate activities to the students who have already mastered the skills.

# CURRICULUM COMPACTOR ASSESSMENT

## Alternate Activities
## Grammar Skills – Adjectives and Adverbs

Alternate Activities should be more challenging than those done by students who are learning the skills or material. You may incorporate points into this assessment or use it as feedback to the student without points. Remember, students working on Alternate Activities in a Compactor have already demonstrated mastery of the skills. Their final grade should reflect that mastery plus the work done on the Alternate Activities.

**1. PowerPoint Presentation**

____Follows PowerPoint criteria card
____Slides have 5 sentences with adjective clauses
____Slides have 5 sentences with adverb clauses
____Sentences need punctuation but it is not there

Comments:

**2. Poem**

____Follows Poem criteria card
____Poem is humorous
____Explains how to identify adjective and adverb clauses
____Explains how to punctuate adjective and adverb clauses
____Oral recitation is understandable, well articulated, and has expression

Comments:

**3. Poster**

____Follows Poster criteria card
____Shows how and when to use comparative and superlative forms
____Gives at least 5 examples of each

Comments:

**4. Brochure**

____Follows Brochure criteria card
____Shows at least 5 common mistakes
____Has several reminders/hints about how not to make these mistakes

Comments:

# CURRICULUM COMPACTOR

## Grammar Skills – Parts of Speech

**Anchor Standard: LA/Language: Conventions of Standard English**

**Common Core Standard:**

- Demonstrate command of the conventions of standard English grammar and usage when writing or speaking.

**Student's Name** ________________________________

| Skill/Knowledge/ Content | Documentation of Mastery | Student Choice Alternate Activities |
|---|---|---|
| Identify the part of speech of a word as used in a given sentence. | 95% correct on parts of speech the pre-test | 1. Create a Mad Lib (a story with blanks for words that are different parts of speech). Try out your Mad Lib with the class filling in the blanks. Have several classmates read theirs aloud. Listen carefully to make sure they have used the correct parts of speech in each blank.<br><br>2. Find a book that has strong and exciting verbs. Write at least 20 of these verbs on a piece of paper along with another verb that you could use to express the same idea. Read your favorite paragraph to the class, emphasizing the verbs.<br><br>3. For nouns, verbs, adjectives, and adverbs, make a list of 10 boring words using each of these parts of speech. Beside each boring word write an exciting word that has a similar meaning.<br><br>4. Make a list of 20 words. Look up each one in the dictionary to see what part or parts of speech they are. When a word can be used as more than one part of speech, write a sentence showing each way it can be used. If it can be only be used as one part of speech, show how you can change it to make it another part of speech. |

** Perpetual alternate activity: Read a book at or above your reading level. Keep a list of words that you don't know. Look them up, and write the definition, part of speech, and an example sentence.*

Note: This standard is a Common Core Anchor Standard and covers all grammar instruction K-12. Use this format with any grammar skills and give higher-level alternate activities to the students who have already mastered the skills.

# CURRICULUM COMPACTOR ASSESSMENT

## Alternate Activities
## Grammar Skills – Parts of Speech

Alternate Activities should be more challenging than those done by students who are learning the skills or material. You may incorporate points into this assessment or use it as feedback to the student without points. Remember, students working on Alternate Activities in a Compactor have already demonstrated mastery of the skills. Their final grade should reflect that mastery plus the work done on the Alternate Activities.

**1. Mad Lib**

____Story has a plot with a beginning, middle and end
____Has at least 2 blanks for each part of speech
____Shares Mad Lib with class
____Gives accurate feedback to classmates about their uses of parts of speech

Comments:

**2. Paragraph Reading**

____Has a total of 40 verbs, 20 from the book and 20 synonyms
____Accurate choice of synonyms
____Oral reading is understandable, well articulated, and has expression
____Verbs are emphasized throughout your reading

Comments:

**3. List**

____Has a list of 10 boring nouns, 10 boring verbs, 10 boring adjectives, and 10 boring adverbs
____Has a corresponding word for each with a similar meaning
____Synonym or similar words are accurate
____Synonyms are more exciting words

Comments:

**4. List with Sentences**

____Has a list of 20 words
____Identifies parts of speech for each word
____Sentences show ways words can be used when they are more than one part of speech
____Sentences show how words can be changed to be different parts of speech

Comments:

# CURRICULUM COMPACTOR

## Grammar Skills – Regular and Irregular Verbs

**Anchor Standard: LA/Language: Conventions of Standard English**

**Common Core Standards:**

- Demonstrate command of the conventions of standard English grammar and usage when writing or speaking.*
- Correctly use frequently confused words.
- Form and use regular and irregular verbs.

**Student's Name** ________________________________

| Skill/Knowledge/ Content | Documentation of Mastery | Student Choice Alternate Activities |
|---|---|---|
| Use regular and irregular verbs correctly using present tense, past tense, and past participles. | 90% correct on the pre-test | 1. Choose a passage from a book that you like, and write a "translation" of at least 10 lines from present to past tense or vice versa.<br>Read your "translation" and analyze how these changes affect the meaning of the passage.<br>Write your conclusions in a paragraph.<br><br>2. Write a funny story using the verbs *sit, set, lie, lay, rise, and raise* correctly.<br><br>3. Make a 3-column chart showing the present tense, past tense, and past participle of 10 irregular verbs.<br>Write a poem using all 30 of these words.<br><br>4. Draw a comic strip with at least 10 frames.<br>Have one character in the comic strip use verbs incorrectly and the other character in the comic strip correct him without using insults. |

*Note: This standard is a Common Core Anchor Standard and covers all grammar instruction K-12. Use this format with any grammar skills and give higher-level alternate activities to the students who have already mastered the skills.

# CURRICULUM COMPACTOR ASSESSMENT

## Alternate Activities
## Grammar Skills – Regular and Irregular Verbs

Alternate Activities should be more challenging than those done by students who are learning the skills or material. You may incorporate points into this assessment or use it as feedback to the student without points. Remember, students working on Alternate Activities in a Compactor have already demonstrated mastery of the skills. Their final grade should reflect that mastery plus the work done on the Alternate Activities.

**1. Translation & Paragraph**

____Changes tenses of verbs in passage from present to past or vice-versa
____Uses at least 10 lines of the passage
____Paragraph analyzes how these changes affect the meaning of the passage

Comments:

**2. Short Story**

____Has a beginning, middle, and end
____Story is funny
____Uses *sit, set, lie, lay, rise* and *raise* correctly

Comments:

**3. Chart and Poem**

____Follows Chart criteria card
____Chart shows present, past, and participles of 10 irregular verbs
____Follows Poem criteria card
____Poem uses all 30 words from the chart

Comments:

**4. Comic Strip**

____Follows Comic Strip criteria card
____Has at least 10 frames
____Has one character who uses verbs incorrectly
____Has one character who corrects incorrect grammar

Comments:

## CURRICULUM COMPACTOR

### Linear Equations

**Math Domain: Functions/Interpreting Functions**

**Common Core Standard:**

- Graph linear and quadratic functions and show intercepts, maxima, and minima.

**Student's Name** ___________________________________

| Skill/Knowledge/ Content | Documentation of Mastery | Student Choice Alternate Activities |
|---|---|---|
| Use the Slope-Intercept form of linear equations | 90% accuracy on the pre-test | 1. Create a PowerPoint presentation showing how to write linear equations from a given slope and y-intercept and how to graph the line from its Slope-Intercept form.<br><br>2. Create a game using the Slope-Intercept form of linear equations. |
| Use the Point-Slope form of linear equations. | 90% accuracy on the pre-test | 3. Design an illustrated flowchart showing how to write linear equations from a given slope and point and how to graph a line from its Point-Slope form.<br><br>4. Design flash cards that would help teach linear equations. |
| Real life applications of linear functions | 90% accuracy on the pre-test including accuracy in short answers about real life applications | 5. Create a collage showing different kinds of linear functions in real life.<br><br>6. Go to the Internet and find three examples of linear functions used in industry. Summarize your findings, and give an oral report to the class. |

# CURRICULUM COMPACTOR ASSESSMENT

## Alternate Activities
## Linear Equations

Alternate Activities should be more challenging than those done by students who are learning the skills or material. You may incorporate points into this assessment or use it as feedback to the student without points. Remember, students working on Alternate Activities in a Compactor have already demonstrated mastery of the skills. Their final grade should reflect that mastery plus the work done on the Alternate Activities.

**1.PowerPoint Presentation**
____Follows PowerPoint criteria card
____Shows how to write linear equations from a given slope and y intercept
____Shows how to graph the line from its Slope-Intercept form
____Clear explanation
Comments:

**2.Game**
____Follows Game criteria card
____Game uses and/or teaches the Slope/Intercept form of linear equations
Comments:

**3. Flowchart**
____Follows Flowchart criteria card
____Shows how to write linear equations from a given slope and point
____Shows how to graph a line from its Point-Slope form
____Illustrations on the flowchart clarify and enhance the information
Comments:

**4. Flash Cards**
____Some flash cards have a linear equation problem on one side and the solution on the other
____One flash card shows example of the Slope Intercept Form of linear equations
____Some flash cards have the Point-Slope form of linear equations
____Each flash card is clear and helpful in understanding linear equations
____Some flash cards use graphs to illustrate given equations
Comments:

**5. Collage**
____Follows Collage criteria card
____Shows at least 3 examples of linear functions
____Illustrates how linear functions are used in the "real world"
____Has labels and formulas
Comments:

**6. Oral Report**
____Follows Oral Report criteria card
____Cites at least three Internet sources
____Has three examples of linear functions used in industry
____Includes illustrations and examples in the report
Comments:

# CURRICULUM COMPACTOR

## Map Skills

**Anchor Standard: Language Arts/Reading: Integration of Knowledge and Ideas**

**Common Core Standard:**

- Integrate and evaluate content presented in diverse formats and media, including visually and quantitatively as well as in words.

**Student's Name** ________________________________

| Skill/Knowledge/ Content | Documentation of Mastery | Student Choice Alternate Activities |
|---|---|---|
| Using a world map with no labels, student is able to identify and label the following: Equator, Prime Meridian, International Date Line, Tropic of Cancer, Tropic of Capricorn, Arctic Circle, Antarctic Circle, and certain given lines of latitude and longitude. | 90% accuracy on the map test | 1. Using a world map, find 10 world capitals. Then use a blank world map that only has lines of longitude and latitude to identify and mark the capitals. On a separate sheet of paper, write the location of each capital using its latitude and longitude. Make a quiz for your classmates indicating the longitude and latitude locations. Include an answer key!<br><br>2. Create a new planet. Draw a map showing important locations and landforms. Write a paragraph describing what this planet is like. |
| Using a world map with no labels, identify and label all seven continents, five oceans, and the Mediterranean Sea. | 90% accuracy (misses one item or less) | 3. On a large poster board, draw a map of the world. Do this freehand without using any references. Label everything you can think of including continents, oceans, other bodies of water, landforms, countries, important landmarks, etc. When you have finished, look at a map and write an evaluation of how well you did. Be specific, evaluating yourself on size, location, shape, what you remembered to include, what you left out, etc.<br><br>4. Draw a map putting the South Pole at the top, the North Pole at the bottom and the Pacific Ocean and Australia in the middle. Include all continents and oceans and all important lines of longitude and latitude such as the Equator, Prime Meridian, and International Date Line. |

# CURRICULUM COMPACTOR ASSESSMENT

## Alternate Activities
## Map Skills

Alternate Activities should be more challenging than those done by students who are learning the skills or material. You may incorporate points into this assessment or use it as feedback to the student without points. Remember, students working on Alternate Activities in a Compactor have already demonstrated mastery of the skills. Their final grade should reflect that mastery plus the work done on the Alternate Activities.

**1. Identification of Locations using Latitude and Longitude**

____Uses a blank world map with lines of longitude and latitude indicated
____Has 10 capitals marked by latitude and longitude instead of their names
____Has an answer key with the names of the capitals and their latitude and longitude
____Creates a quiz for classmates using this information

Comments:

**2. New Planet**

____Follows Map criteria card
____New planet has a name and basic information about what it is like
____Locations and landforms are indicated on the map
____Paragraph gives information about the planet that correlates with what is on the map

Comments:

**3. Map of the World**

____Is drawn freehand without consulting any references
____Includes continents, oceans, other bodies of water, landforms, countries, and important landmarks
____Written evaluation is specific as to accuracy of the drawing, what was left out, etc.

Comments:

**4. Upside Down Map**

____Follows Map criteria card
____South Pole is at the top and the North Pole is at the bottom
____Pacific Ocean and Australia are in the middle
____Includes all continents and oceans and important lines of latitude and longitude

Comments:

## CURRICULUM COMPACTOR
## Multiplication, Division and Fractions

**Math Domain: Number and Operations – Fractions; Geometry**

**Common Core Standards:**
- Find whole number quotients and remainders with up to four-digit dividends and one-digit divisors.
- Apply and extend previous understandings of multiplication and division to multiply and divide fractions.
- Solve real world mathematical problems.

**Student's Name** ____________________________

| Skill/Knowledge/ Content | Documentation of Mastery | Student Choice Alternate Activities |
|---|---|---|
| Dividing by a smaller divisor than dividend<br><br>Multiplying and dividing fractions | 90% accuracy on the pre-test | 1. Using division, figure out the batting average of each player on your favorite baseball team. Round the batting average to the thousandth place. Then list the players from greatest to least batting average.<br><br>2. Create an oral presentation that demonstrates to your class how to multiply and divide fractions. Make sure you assume that your audience does not know how to do this. Use multiple visual and/or digital representations and examples to assist them in further understanding.<br><br>3. Plan a 14-day summer road trip for your family. You must plan to visit at least 5 states. You need to select the vehicle that your family will travel in and then find out the number of gallons of gas that it will take for the entire trip as well as the cost of gas per gallon. Complete a chart to indicate your starting point, each stopping point, miles traveled per day, and the cost of gas per day. Use www.mapquest.com to help you plan your trip and to get information on the distances from one place to another. |

# CURRICULUM COMPACTOR ASSESSMENT

## Alternate Activities
## Multiplication, Division and Fractions

Alternate Activities should be more challenging than those done by students who are learning the skills or material. You may incorporate points into this assessment or use it as feedback to the student without points. Remember, students working on Alternate Activities in a Compactor have already demonstrated mastery of the skills. Their final grade should reflect that mastery plus the work done on the Alternate Activities.

**1. Baseball Batting Averages**

____Figures batting average of at least 10 players
____Batting averages for each are to the thousandth place
____Has a list of players from best to worst batting average
____Accurate computation

Comments:

**2. Oral Presentation with Visuals**

____Follows Oral Presentation criteria card
____The process of how to multiply and divide fractions is clearly explained
____Uses multiple visuals (digital or drawn) to help explain concepts
____Has several examples that show how to multiply and divide fractions

Comments:

**3. Plan for Road Trip**

____Follows Chart criteria card
____Plan is for 14 days
____Shows plans to visit 5 or more states
____Vehicle selection noted
____Amounts of gas and cost calculated correctly
____Chart indicates starting point, stopping points, miles traveled, and cost of gas

Comments:

# CURRICULUM COMPACTOR

## Numbers and Counting

**Math Domain: Number and Operations in Base 10**

**Common Core Standards:**

- Count to 120, starting at any number less than 120. In this range, read and write numerals and represent a number of objects with a written numeral.
- Integrate and evaluate information presented in diverse media and formats, including visually, quantitatively and orally.

**Student's Name** ________________________________

| Skill/Knowledge/ Content | Documentation of Mastery | Student Choice Alternate Activities |
|---|---|---|
| Equate a number word's written name and its numerical form up to number 120.<br><br>Count and show the number of objects that correspond to a written numeral. | 90% accuracy on the pre-test | 1. Create a collage of 20 examples of a number's written name and its numerical form.<br>Use any two- or three-digit numbers up to 120.<br><br>2. Locate 5 places in your state that are not more than 120 miles from where you live.<br>Find the distance for each.<br>Write the name of each place.<br>Then write the distance in word form and numerical form.<br><br>3. Make a chart with 12 sections.<br>Put a number in each section using one-, two-, and three-digit numbers up to 120.<br>Then show the number of objects that correspond to each of your chosen numbers. |

## CURRICULUM COMPACTOR ASSESSMENT

### Alternate Activities
### Numbers and Counting

Alternate Activities should be more challenging than those done by students who are learning the skills or material. You may incorporate points into this assessment or use it as feedback to the student without points. Remember, students working on Alternate Activities in a Compactor have already demonstrated mastery of the skills. Their final grade should reflect that mastery plus the work done on the Alternate Activities.

**1. Collage**

____Follows Collage criteria card
____Has 20 examples in the collage
____Each example has the written name and the numeral for the number

Comments:

**2. Locations and Distances**

____Lists the names of five places in your state
____Each place is no more than 120 miles away
____Next to the name of the place is the distance in word form and numerical form

*Suggested extension:*
*Get a road map, and highlight the way you could go to each of these places.*

Comments:

**3. Chart**

____Follows Chart criteria card
____Chart has 12 sections
____Has a number in each section
____Number of objects in each section is correct for the number shown

Comments:

# CURRICULUM COMPACTOR

## Perspective

**Math Domain: Geometry**
**Anchor Standard: LA/Speaking and Listening: Presentation of Knowledge and Ideas**

**Common Core Standards:**

- Draw, construct and describe geometrical figures and describe the relationships between them.
- Solve real life mathematical problems involving angle measure, area, surface area and volume.
- Make strategic use of digital media and visual displays of data to express information and enhance understanding of presentations.

**Student's Name** ________________________________

| Skill/Knowledge/ Content | Documentation of Mastery | Student Choice Alternate Activities |
|---|---|---|
| Identify linear and aerial perspective in several pieces of artwork from print and online sources. | Identify both linear and aerial perspective in a variety of artworks with 90% accuracy | Continue to the linear perspective activity below. |
| Create architectural structures in realistic detail using linear perspective. | Accurately draw a picture with three buildings using appropriate linear perspective, including overlapping, sizing, and strips | 1. Create a cityscape using two-point perspective with 3 buildings.<br>or<br>2. Create a cityscape of a particular present-day location or a location in a certain historical time. |
| Create architectural structures in realistic detail using aerial perspective. | Illustrate aerial perspective by successfully completing a sketch that shows this type of perspective | 3. Create a series of landscape and cityscape drawings from the point of view of a person in an airplane.<br>or<br>4. Log onto http://sketchup.google.com and use it to do a three-dimensional drawing using aerial perspective. |

# CURRICULUM COMPACTOR ASSESSMENT

## Alternate Activities
## Perspective

Alternate Activities should be more challenging than those done by students who are learning the skills or material. You may incorporate points into this assessment or use it as feedback to the student without points. Remember, students working on Alternate Activities in a Compactor have already demonstrated mastery of the skills. Their final grade should reflect that mastery plus the work done on the Alternate Activities.

**1. Cityscape in Two-Point Perspective**

____Correctly uses 2-point perspective
____Drawing has at least three buildings
____Obvious to viewer that this is a scene in a city
____Has other objects in drawing such as a road, river, bridge, shopping mall, etc.

Comments:

**2. Cityscape of a Particular Location**

____Correctly uses 2-point perspective
____Location is indicated/labeled along with approximate date
____Accurately portrays present-day scene or historical scene
____Has at least two buildings plus other interesting objects in the scene

Comments:

**3. Landscapes and Cityscapes from an Airplane**

____Has at least 3 drawings
____All drawings show aerial perspective
____Accurate depiction of a landscape or cityscape from an airplane
____Approximate distance from the ground is noted

Comments:

**4. Aerial Drawing using Google Sketch up**

____Logs onto appropriate website and correctly navigates it
____Uses appropriate tools from website to create a three-dimensional drawing
____Drawing shows an aerial perspective of a building or scene

Comments:

# CURRICULUM COMPACTOR

## Root Words, Prefixes and Suffixes

**Anchor Standard: LA/Language: Conventions of Standard English**
**Anchor Standard: LA/Language: Vocabulary Acquisition and Use**

**Common Core Standards:**

- Demonstrate command of the conventions of standard English grammar and usage when writing or speaking.*
- Use common, grade-appropriate Greek and Latin affixes and roots as clues to the meaning of a word.

**Student's Name** ____________________________

| Skill/Knowledge/ Content | Documentation of Mastery | Student Choice Alternate Activities |
|---|---|---|
| Determines the meaning of unfamiliar words using knowledge of common roots, suffixes, and prefixes. | 90% accuracy on pre-test covering root words, prefixes, and suffixes | 1. Create an illustrated 20-page booklet showing 10 suffixes, 10 prefixes, and their meanings. Include examples of at least five words that use each prefix and each suffix. Use one page for each prefix and suffix.<br><br>2. Make a list of 10 root words. Define each and include their derivation or what language they came from originally. Then list 5 words that come from each of your root words.<br><br>3. Design a poster with at least 5 word webs on it. On each web, put the root word in the middle, prefixes or suffixes on the lines leading to the outer circles of the web, and a new word created from combining the root word with the prefix or suffix in each outer circle. |

*Note: This standard is a Common Core Anchor Standard and covers all grammar instruction K-12. Use this format with any grammar skills and give higher-level alternate activities to the students who have already mastered the skills.

# CURRICULUM COMPACTOR ASSESSMENT

## Alternate Activities
## Root Words, Prefixes and Suffixes

Alternate Activities should be more challenging than those done by students who are learning the skills or material. You may incorporate points into this assessment or use it as feedback to the student without points. Remember, students working on Alternate Activities in a Compactor have already demonstrated mastery of the skills. Their final grade should reflect that mastery plus the work done on the Alternate Activities.

**1. Booklet**

____Has 10 prefixes and their meanings, one per page
____Has 10 suffixes and their meanings, one per page
____Each page is illustrated
____Each page has at least 5 words that use the prefix or suffix

Comments:

**2. List and Definitions**

____Has a list of 10 root words
____Each root word has a definition and a derivation
____Has 5 words that come from each root word

Comments:

**3. Poster**

____Poster has 5 word webs
____Each word web has a root word in the middle
____Each word web has prefixes or suffixes on lines leading from the middle to outer circles
____Outer circles have words created from the root word and the prefix or suffix

Comments:

# CURRICULUM COMPACTOR

## Rotations, Reflections and Translations

**Math Domain: Congruence**

**Common Core Standards:**

- Given a rectangle, parallelogram, trapezoid or regular polygon, describe the rotations and reflections that carry it onto itself.
- Develop definitions of rotations, reflections and translations in terms of angles, circles, perpendicular lines, parallel lines and line segments.
- Given a geometric figure and a rotation, reflection or translation, draw the transformed figure. Specify a sequence of transformations that will carry a given figure onto another.

**Student's Name** ______________________________

| Skill/Knowledge Content | Documentation of Mastery | Student Choice Alternate Activities |
|---|---|---|
| Can define rotation, reflection, and translation using several geometric lines and figures.<br><br>Use the concepts of rotation, proportion, and scale factor to demonstrate the relationships between several geometric figures. | 95% mastery in a pre-test of the following:<br><br>• identifying rotations, reflections, and translations<br><br>• identifying degrees of rotation in angles, circles, perpendicular lines, parallel lines, and line segments | 1. Measure the height and width of your room, and determine the scale factor to create a scale drawing for your room. Your drawing should include angles, circles, perpendicular lines, parallel lines, and line segments.<br><br>2. Design a PowerPoint presentation showing the rotations that result with a rectangle, parallelogram, trapezoid, or regular polygon.<br><br>3. Begin with one geometric figure. Draw a logo for a school banner or T-shirt that uses this figure and a sequence of transformations. You can draw this on graph paper or tracing paper, or you can use a computer drawing program. |

# CURRICULUM COMPACTOR ASSESSMENT

## Alternate Activities
## Rotations, Reflections and Translations

Alternate Activities should be more challenging than those done by students who are learning the skills or material. You may incorporate points into this assessment or use it as feedback to the student without points. Remember, students working on Alternate Activities in a Compactor have already demonstrated mastery of the skills. Their final grade should reflect that mastery plus the work done on the Alternate Activities.

**1. Scale Drawing**

____Follows Drawing criteria card
____Accurate measurement of the room
____Scale drawing is done to scale based on the measurements
____Drawing includes angles, circles, perpendicular lines, parallel lines, and line segments
____Each of the above is labeled or indicated in some way

Comments:

**2. PowerPoint Presentation**

____Follows PowerPoint criteria card
____Animations accurately show rotations
____Results of rotations create a rectangle, parallelogram, trapezoid, or regular polygon
____Presentation given to class and class questions accurately answered

Comments:

**3. Logo**

____Begins with one geometric figure
____Logo is created from this figure and a sequence of transformations
____Logo is neat, colorful, and visually attractive

*Suggested extension: Make a banner or some T-shirts with your logo on them.*

Comments:

# CURRICULUM COMPACTOR

## Sentence Structure

**Anchor Standard: LA/Language: Conventions of Standard English**

**Common Core Standards:**

- Demonstrate command of the conventions of standard English grammar and usage when writing or speaking.
- Demonstrate command of the conventions of standard English capitalization, punctuation, and spelling when writing.

**Student's Name** ________________________________

| Skill/Knowledge/ Content | Documentation of Mastery | Student Choice Alternate Activities |
|---|---|---|
| Identify and write simple, compound, complex, and compound-complex sentences correctly. Capitalize and punctuate properly, avoiding fragments, run-on sentences, and combining sentences incorrectly. | 90% accuracy on the pre-test | 1. Write a story that uses at least 3 of each of the four types of sentences correctly.<br>Use four different highlighters to highlight each type.<br><br>2. Make a flip book that shows how to distinguish the differences between the four different types of sentences.<br>Include definitions and explanations on one side of the flip book and examples on the corresponding page.<br><br>3. Write a silly story where you use incorrect punctuation, fragments, and run-on sentences.<br>Then rewrite the same story using correct English grammar.<br><br>4. Make a foldable with two sides.<br>On the left write 10 simple sentences.<br>On the right, use these sentences to write compound, complex, and compound-complex sentences that combine as many simple sentences as possible. |

# CURRICULUM COMPACTOR ASSESSMENT

## Alternate Activities
## Sentence Structure

Alternate Activities should be more challenging than those done by students who are learning the skills or material. You may incorporate points into this assessment or use it as feedback to the student without points. Remember, students working on Alternate Activities in a Compactor have already demonstrated mastery of the skills. Their final grade should reflect that mastery plus the work done on the Alternate Activities.

**1. Story**

____Story has a beginning, middle, and end
____Uses at least three of each of these: simple sentence, compound sentence, complex sentence, and compound-complex sentence
____Each type of sentence is indicated in some way (such as color-coding types of sentences using different colors of highlighters or different colored fonts)

Comments:

**2. Flip Book**

____Follows Flip Book criteria card
____Has a page for each of the four types of sentences
____Includes definitions and explanations on one page
____Has examples on the corresponding page

Comments:

**3. Silly Story**

____Story is humorous and has a beginning, middle, and end
____Story uses incorrect punctuation, sentence fragments, and run-on sentences
____Story is rewritten correctly

Comments:

**4. Foldable with Two Sides**

____Uses paper that is folded in half
____Has 10 simple sentences on the left side of the paper
____Uses these simple sentences to form the compound, complex, and compound-complex sentences written on the right side of the paper

Comments:

# CURRICULUM COMPACTOR

______________________________ (Topic)

**Common Core Standards:**

**Student's Name** ________________________________

| Skill/Knowledge/ Content | Documentation of Mastery | Student Choice Alternate Activities |
|---|---|---|
| | | |

## CURRICULUM COMPACTOR ASSESSMENT

### Alternate Activities

________________________________(Topic)

Alternate Activities should be more challenging than those done by students who are learning the skills or material. You may incorporate points into this assessment or use it as feedback to the student without points. Remember, students working on Alternate Activities in a Compactor have already demonstrated mastery of the skills. Their final grade should reflect that mastery plus the work done on the Alternate Activities.

**1.** ________________________________ **(Activity)**

____
____
____
____

Comments:

**2.** ________________________________ **(Activity)**

____
____
____
____

Comments:

**3.** ________________________________ **(Activity)**

____
____
____
____

Comments:

**4.** ________________________________ **(Activity)**

____
____
____
____

Comments:

# INDIVIDUAL LESSON PLAN™

## INDIVIDUAL LESSON PLAN (ILP™) FORMAT

The **ILP**™ format is a graphic organizer used to design a unit of work. It organizes standards-based learning activities so that students have a choice as to which activities they want to do. These choices can be based on student Learning Profiles or Preferences such as learning styles, learning modalities or multiple intelligences. They can also be based on subject areas, Bloom's Taxonomy, different aspects of the standard or content, or any other way that creates categories of student choices.

The **ILP**™ format explains what the students are going to do and what learning choices they have. It does not necessarily tell everything the teacher is going to do. Even though it outlines an entire unit of work, this format is called an **Individual Lesson Plan** because each student uses it to create his or her own individual lesson plan for the unit by choosing one or more of the *Student Choice Activities*. For students in grades 3-12, offer no more than eight *Student Choice Activities*. In another section of this book is the **Primary ILP**™ to use for grades K-2. This form often has only four choices. (See page 87 for more information.)

The **ILP**™ form has a place in the middle of the form to list the standards addressed in the unit. In writing Individual Lesson Plans for this book, it was quickly evident that each one undoubtedly dealt with at least six or seven of the Common Core Standards. Some addressed many more. The form is designed to note two or three standards so that is what appears. In nearly every case, however, there are several additional standards that could have been used. When you use my ILP™ units, feel free to change the Common Core Standards indicated. You can make use of the same unit and replace the standards. Those noted are those you want to emphasize!

In addition to *Student Choice Activities*, which are listed in boxes to the left of the black vertical line on the form, the upper right hand quadrant of the **ILP**™ lists the *Teacher Required Activities* that all students must do. This combination of *Student Choice* and *Teacher Required* activities makes up a differentiated unit of work.

The first *Teacher Required Activity* should be an independent activity for students. Students can work on this activity while the teacher is meeting with small groups of students regarding each *Student Choice* activity. The other *Teacher Required Activities* usually are teacher directed whole class activities that will be done during the course of the unit.

The *Student Choice Activities* are numbered and the students write the numbers to indicate their choices on the bottom middle block of the **ILP**™ form. On the next block to the right, each student lists the products or performances he or she will produce as a result of doing their chosen activities. The block on the far right shows the due dates for each of the individual *Student Choice* activities.

The teacher decides how many *Student Choice Activities* each student must do. Often teachers begin by requiring students to make two choices, each from a different category. If students finish early, they can make an additional choice. Sometimes teachers only have time to give the student one choice. This is also okay. Use the form to best suit your teaching situation and the time you have available.

To know which activities each of the students in your class has chosen, use an Activity Chart to record the choices each student makes. Call the roll and have each student answer with the numbers of his or her choices. My policy is that once the choices are recorded on the Activity Chart, students cannot change their minds. This encourages careful selection and teaches both commitment and responsibility.

An example Activity Chart is on page 66. Use the blank Activity Chart (page 67) to list your students and record their choices. You can also customize the blank form on the CD.

Use the Activity Chart to find out which students have chosen the same activity. Meet with all students who are doing the same activity to review assessment criteria, due dates, etc. For some choices (such as a skit or debate) these students will need to work together. Meet with small groups of students for each of the *Student Choice Activities*. You can write the due dates for each activity on the Activity Chart. While you are doing this, students you are not currently meeting with should be working on *Teacher Required Activity* #1.

Plan the due dates carefully. Activities such as debates or oral reports need class time for preparation and presentation. Make sure everything is not due on the same day! This avoids student procrastination and makes grading less overwhelming for you. It helps to distribute these events throughout the week or weeks the students are working. It also assures oral reports and other classroom presentations are spaced over several days.

Assessing the Student Choice Activities could be an arduous task if we chose to write a complex rubric for all eight student choices! For that reason, Mini-Rubrics correspond with each student choice activity. These list the criteria for each student activity. Many contain criteria cards as part of the assessment criteria. Most also include an extension for those who want to extend their learning further.

Individual Lesson Plans with corresponding assessments in this section of the book include:



At the end of this section, you will find a blank Individual Lesson Plan form and a blank Individual Lesson Plan Assessment form to use as you write your own.

## Anchor Standards for ILPs™

**Engineering Careers p. 68**

Language Arts/Writing: Production and Distribution of Writing
Language Arts/Literacy in History, Social Studies, Science and Technical Subjects: Integration of Knowledge and Ideas

**Industrial Revolution p. 70**

Language Arts/Literacy in History, Social Studies Science and Technical Subjects: Range of Reading; Level of Text Complexity
Language Arts/Literacy in History, Social Studies, Science and Technical Subjects: Speaking and Listening: Presentation of Knowledge and Ideas
Language Arts/Literacy in History, Social Studies, Science and Technical Subjects: Writing: Research to Build and Present Knowledge

**The Rise of Democratic Ideas p. 72**

Language Arts/Literacy in History, Social Studies, Science and Technical Subjects: Range of Reading; Level of Text Complexity
Language Arts/Literacy in History, Social Studies, Science and Technical Subjects: Speaking and Listening: Presentation of Knowledge and Ideas
Language Arts/Literacy in History, Social Studies, Science and Technical Subjects: Writing: Research to Build and Present Knowledge

**Scientific Classification/Six Kingdoms p. 74**

Language Arts/Literacy in History, Social Studies, Science and Technical Subjects: Speaking and Listening: Presentation of Knowledge and Ideas
Language Arts/Literacy in History, Social Studies, Science and Technical Subjects: Writing: Research to Build and Present Knowledge

**Sea Turtles p. 76**

Language Arts/Literacy in History, Social Studies, Science and Technical Subjects
Reading: Range of Reading; Level of Text Complexity
Language Arts/Language: Vocabulary Acquisition and Use
Language Arts/Writing: Production and Distribution of Writing

**Statistics and Probability p.78**

Math: Interpreting Categorical and Quantitative Data
Math: Using Probability to Make Decisions

**Using the Internet p. 80**

Language Arts/Reading: Integration of Knowledge and Ideas
Language Arts/Writing: Production and Distribution of Writing

**Volcanoes p. 82**

Language Arts/Writing: Production and Distribution of Writing
Language Arts/Reading: Integration of Knowledge and Ideas

## Activity Chart

### Student Choice Activities

| Students' Names | 1 | 2 | 3 | 4 | 5 | 6 | 7 | 8 |
|---|---|---|---|---|---|---|---|---|
| Alicia | | ✓ | | | ✓ | | | |
| Carlos | | | | ✓ | | | ✓ | |
| Danielle | ✓ | | | | | ✓ | | |
| Evan | | | ✓ | | | | | ✓ |
| Edwardo | | | | ✓ | | ✓ | | |
| Gina | | ✓ | | | | | ✓ | |
| Heather | | | | | ✓ | | ✓ | |
| Jim | | | ✓ | | | ✓ | | |
| Kara | ✓ | | | | | | | ✓ |
| Maria | | | ✓ | | | ✓ | | |
| Mark | | ✓ | | | ✓ | | | |
| Nathan | ✓ | | | | | ✓ | | |
| Ophra | | | ✓ | | | | | ✓ |
| Paul | | ✓ | | | | ✓ | | |
| Pedro | | | | ✓ | | | ✓ | |
| Quintan | ✓ | | | | | | | ✓ |
| Rachel | | | | ✓ | | ✓ | | |
| Rusty | | | | | ✓ | | ✓ | |
| Sarah | ✓ | | | ✓ | | | | |
| Taneka | | ✓ | | | | | | ✓ |
| Tom | | | | ✓ | | | ✓ | |

Using this chart helps teachers organize a differentiated classroom. Each student in this example chose 2 activities from the 8 Student Choice Activities available. Each child's choices are recorded by using the number that corresponds to the activity.

The teacher meets with each group of students. At this time, review the assessment criteria, explain the activity, and schedule the due date. Record the due date on the chart and also write it in the teacher's plan book. If the activity is one that requires students working together, review behavioral guidelines with the students involved.

### Activity Chart
## Student Choice Activities

| Students' Names | 1 | 2 | 3 | 4 | 5 | 6 | 7 | 8 |
|---|---|---|---|---|---|---|---|---|
| | | | | | | | | |
| | | | | | | | | |
| | | | | | | | | |
| | | | | | | | | |
| | | | | | | | | |
| | | | | | | | | |
| | | | | | | | | |
| | | | | | | | | |
| | | | | | | | | |
| | | | | | | | | |
| | | | | | | | | |
| | | | | | | | | |
| | | | | | | | | |
| | | | | | | | | |
| | | | | | | | | |
| | | | | | | | | |
| | | | | | | | | |
| | | | | | | | | |
| | | | | | | | | |
| | | | | | | | | |
| | | | | | | | | |

**Notes**

## Individual Lesson Plan™ Engineering Careers

### ACTIVITIES – STUDENT CHOICES

| Visual | Interpersonal |
|---|---|
| 1. Choose one type of engineering career. Create a **chart** showing Type of Work, Education Needed, Salary, Examples of Things Built, and Other Information.<br><br>2. Choose a major engineering project such as the building of a dam or bridge or designing a rocket. Make a **time line** from the conception of the project to its finish. Identify the types of engineers who worked on the project at each stage and what each type did. | 3. Find someone in your neighborhood, place of worship, or school who is an engineer. Ask this person to come to school and talk to your class. Give him/her at least **5 questions** to answer about his career. Set up the **date and time** for this talk to your class.<br><br>4. Give an **oral report** about a female engineer. Include how she became an engineer, her work, and obstacles she faced. Answer questions about this person. |
| **Technological** | **Kinesthetic** |
| 5. Log onto www.pbs.org/wgbh/buildingbig/profile/index. Choose one of the engineers featured. Read his/ her biography and do a **PowerPoint presentation** summarizing the 10 most important things you learned about this person.<br><br>6. Log onto www.pbs.org/wgbh/buildingbig/profile/career and choose one of the types of engineering careers listed. Do a two-minute **podcast** highlighting what you learned. | 7. Make a **model** of a house, car, bridge, skyscraper, highway, or airplane. Write a **handbook** telling what work different engineers would need to do to make this in the real world.<br><br>8. Create a **bulletin board** showing at least 8 different engineering careers. Include pictures of engineers at work, statistics about education and salaries, and interesting things engineers have made or worked on. |

| Required Activities<br>Teacher's Choice | Product/Performance<br>Required | Assessment<br>Required Activities |
|---|---|---|
| 1. Explore the web site www.discoverengineering.org. Using the information on this web site, **list** and **define** at least 3 types of engineering careers that interest you. | 1. List and definitions | 1. Lists three types of engineering with clear definitions of what each is and the kind of work each engineer does. |
| 2. Aerospace engineer Theodore Von Karman said, "Scientists discover the world that exists. Engineers create the world that never was." Write a **short essay** telling what you think he means. Give examples to support what you say. | 2. Essay with examples | 2. Has clear and coherent writing.<br>Thoughtful and logical explanation of the meaning of the quote.<br>Has at least three examples.<br>Correct grammar, punctuation, and spelling. |

**Common Core Standards:**
- Produce clear and coherent writing in which the development, organization and style are appropriate to task, purpose and audience.
- Integrate and evaluate content presented in diverse formats and media, including visually and quantitatively as well as in words.

| Student Choices in Ways to Learn | Product/Performance<br>Student Choice | Due Dates<br>Student Choice Activities |
|---|---|---|
| Visual | | |
| Interpersonal | | |
| Technological | | |
| Kinesthetic | | |

# Assessment of Student Choices - Individual Lesson Plan – Engineering Careers

**1. Chart (Visual)**
- Follows Chart criteria card
- Focus of chart is one type of engineering career
- Includes Type of Work, Education Needed, Salary, Examples of Things Built, and Other Information
- Accurate information

*Suggested extension: Has additional informational categories on chart.*

Possible points = ______

**2. Time Line (Visual)**
- Follows Time Line criteria card
- Project is an actual project completed sometime in the past
- Includes at least 6 steps from start to finish
- Identifies types of engineers who worked on the project and what each did at each stage

*Suggested extension: Discover the names of some of the engineers and find out what they are doing now.*

Possible points = ______

**3. Five Questions and Organizing a Talk**
- Locates a person who is an engineer and organizes a time for this person to come to the class and talk
- Has five questions about an engineering career that this person will answer
- Introduces person to the class, telling important facts about his/her background

*Suggested extension: Has each member of the class write a thank you note telling what each person learned.*

Possible points = ______

**4. Oral Report (Interpersonal)**
- Follows Oral Report criteria card
- Focuses on a female engineer
- Includes how she became an engineer, her work, and obstacles she faced
- Accurately answers questions from class

*Suggested extension: Creates some type of visual (map, chart, etc.) to go with the report.*

Possible points = ______

**5. PowerPoint Presentation (Technological)**
- Follows PowerPoint criteria card
- Focuses on one engineer
- Shows at least 10 important things about the person and his/her work and accomplishments

*Suggested extension: Write an action plan showing how you could use this person as a model for your life.*

Possible points = ______

**6. Podcast (Technological)**
- Follows Podcast criteria card
- Focuses on one type of engineering career
- Accurate information about chosen type of engineering

*Suggested extension: Connects several other types of engineering to the career focused on.*

Possible points = ______

**7. Model & Handbook (Kinesthetic & Written)**
- Follows Model criteria card
- Model is a house, car, bridge, skyscraper, highway, or airplane
- Handbook gives details on how various types of engineers would work on this in the real world

*Suggested extension: Handbook includes pictures of this item as it is being worked on in the real world.*

Possible points = ______

**8. Bulletin Board (Kinesthetic)**
- Shows at least 8 different engineering careers
- Has pictures of engineers at work & labels of types of engineers
- Has statistics showing education and salaries of engineers
- Shows interesting or unique engineering feats

*Suggested extension: Explains bulletin board to class.*

Possible points = ______

## Individual Lesson Plan™ The Industrial Revolution

### ACTIVITIES – STUDENT CHOICES

| Application | Analysis |
|---|---|
| 1. Research how child labor was used during the Industrial Revolution. Create a **poster** that advocates for abolishing child labor. Be historically accurate for the time period.<br><br>2. Pretend you are Robert Fulton, Eli Whitney, or Francis Cabot Lodge. Write a journal about how your invention and/or factory is changing America. Include at least 5 entries from different time periods. | 3. Design **a T-Chart** listing 10 examples of everyday life before the Industrial Revolution and after the Industrial Revolution. Write a short paragraph comparing the two.<br><br>4. Give an oral report about at least three machines developed during the Industrial Revolution and how they changed life for ordinary people. |
| **Synthesis** | **Evaluation** |
| 5. Log onto http://museumbox.e2bn.org Create a **museum box** with photos, text, film clips, and other information about the Industrial Revolution.<br><br>6. With a group, write and act out a skit about life during the Industrial Revolution. The skit should show at least three aspects of life during this time and should have specific references to actual inventions, factories, hardships, and successes of this time period. | 7. Research information about other countries that use child labor today. Post a **blog** explaining why you think this is wrong. In your blog, compare this to practices during the Industrial Revolution in England and America.<br><br>8. Pretend you are the editor of a newspaper during the 1800s. Write an editorial discussing the pluses and minuses of all the changes taking place due to the Industrial Revolution. |

| Required Activities Teacher's Choice | Product/Performance Required | Assessment Required Activities |
|---|---|---|
| 1. Read basic information about the Industrial Revolution in their text books and answer the assigned questions. | 1. Answers to questions. | 1. Accurate answers. All questions completed. |
| 2. Create a time line starting with the beginning of the Industrial Revolution to the early 20th century. Include at least 10 important events. | 2. Time line. | 2. Follows Time Line criteria card. Begins in the 18th century ad goes to the 20th century. Includes 10 or more events that are connected to the industrial Revolution. |
| 3. Research some aspect of the Industrial Revolution. Write an informative essay explaining its importance and impact on society. | 3. Informative essay. | 3. Uses at least 3 resources. Focuses on one aspect of the Industrial Revolution. Explains importance and impact on society. Clear and organized writing. |

**Common Core Standards:**
- Read and comprehend complex literary and informational texts independently and proficiently.
- Make strategic use of digital media and visual displays of data to express information and enhance understanding of presentations.
- Draw evidence from literary and informational texts to support analysis, reflection and research.

| Student Choices in Ways to Learn | Product/Performance Student Choice | Due Dates Student Choice Activities |
|---|---|---|
| Application | | |
| Analysis | | |
| Synthesis | | |
| Evaluation | | |

## Assessment of Student Choices - Individual Lesson Plan – The Industrial Revolution

| | |
|---|---|
| **1. Poster (Application)**<br>• Follows Poster criteria card<br>• Messages on poster advocate for abolishing child labor<br>• Examples or pictures historically accurate for time period<br>*Suggested extension: Make two posters, one that reflects on conditions in the United States and the other on conditions in England.*<br>Possible points = ______ | **3. T-Chart (Analysis)**<br>• Chart has 2 columns with headings: Before Industrial Revolution & After Industrial Revolution<br>• Has 10 examples on each side of chart<br>• Historically accurate<br>• Paragraph clearly written with evidence comparing the two time periods<br>Possible points = ______ |
| **2. Journal (Application)**<br>• Indicates person whose journal it is<br>• Tells about invention or factory and change in America<br>• Has at least 5 entries from different time periods<br>*Suggested extension: Include actual quotes from this person. You will have to do extra research to find these!*<br>Possible points = ______ | **4. Oral Report (Analysis)**<br>• Follows Oral Report criteria card<br>• Accurate information about three machines developed during the Industrial Revolution<br>• Tells how each of these machines changed life<br>*Suggested extension: Include visuals for each of the machines.*<br>Possible points = ______ |
| **5. Museum Box (Synthesis)**<br>• Uses museum box website to create product<br>• Has photos, text and film clips about the Industrial Revolution<br>• Focuses on at least four different aspects of the Industrial Revolution<br>*Suggested extension: Do a presentation for your class using your museum box.*<br>Possible points = ______ | **7. Blog (Evaluation)**<br>• Follows Blog criteria card<br>• Discusses reasons child labor is wrong<br>• Compares current child labor practices to those during the Industrial Revolution<br>*Suggested extension: Email an American company that uses overseas child labor and explain why you think this is wrong.*<br>Possible points = ______ |
| **6. Skit (Synthesis)**<br>• Follows Skit criteria card<br>• Shows at least three aspects of life during the Industrial Revolution<br>• Has specific references to inventions, factories, hardships, and successes during the Industrial Revolution<br>*Suggested extension: Video this skit and post on YouTube.*<br>Possible points = ______ | **8. Editorial (Evaluation)**<br>• Correct grammar, spelling, and punctuation<br>• Discusses pluses and minuses of the Industrial Revolution<br>• Historically accurate and written from the point of view of an editor in the 1800s<br>*Suggested extension: Write an entire newspaper for this time period.*<br>Possible points = ______ |

# Individual Lesson Plan™ - The Rise of Democratic Ideas

## ACTIVITIES – STUDENT CHOICES

| Application | Synthesis |
|---|---|
| 1. Write a Rap **Song** about the history of democratic ideas. Your song should mention the major founders, main beliefs, written documents, and how these have contributed to democracy. Sing this song to your class.<br>2. Write 5 ideas for your school that follow democratic ideas. Make a **ballot**, and have your class vote on each. Count the votes for and against each idea, and write a **paragraph** explaining what the votes showed. | 5. Write and present a **eulogy** about Pericles, Solon, or Cleisthenes. Make sure you talk about this person's life accomplishments and his contributions to democratic ideas.<br>6. Create an Acrostic **poem** using the word Democracy that highlights the rise of democratic ideas. |
| **Analysis** | **Evaluation** |
| 3. Use a **Venn Diagram** to show similarities and differences in Greek and Roman political thought.<br>4. Make an **oral presentation** explaining the differences between a dictatorship, a constitutional monarchy, and a democracy with an elected president. | 7. Create a **PowerPoint Presentation** about the U.S. Constitution and your evaluation of how well it has worked. Give examples to back up your ideas.<br>8. Make a **list** of five countries that are working on becoming democracies. Design a **chart** to identify three criteria that you think would show progress toward becoming a democratic society, and rate each country based on this criteria. |

| Required Activities Teacher's Choice | Product/Performance Required | Assessment Required Activities |
|---|---|---|
| 1. Read from textbook and other informational texts to gain information about Greek and Roman democratic thought. Take notes on what you read. | 1. Notes from reading | 1. Notes are complete and accurate.<br>Covers information on Greek and Roman thought. |
| 2. Make a time line of the development of democratic thought from Athenian democracy to the present. | 2. Time line | 2. Follows Time line criteria card.<br>Shows at least 10 significant events or documents in the development of democratic thought.<br>Accuracy. |
| 3. Listen to teacher lectures and audio-visual presentations. Participate in class discussion. | 3. Active participation | |

**Common Core Standards:**

- Read and comprehend complex literary and informational texts independently and proficiently.
- Make strategic use of digital media and visual displays of data to express information and enhance understanding of presentations.
- Draw evidence from literary and informational texts to support analysis, reflection and research.

| Student Choices in Ways to Learn | Product/Performance Student Choice | Due Dates Student Choice Activities |
|---|---|---|
| Application | | |
| Analysis | | |
| Synthesis | | |
| Evaluation | | |

## Assessment of Student Choices - Individual Lesson Plan – Rise of Democratic Ideas

| | |
|---|---|
| **1. Rap Song (Application)**<br>• Follows Song criteria card<br>• Includes major founders of democracy (at least 5)<br>• Refers to main beliefs and important documents (at least 5)<br>• Correct information<br>• Sings song to class<br>*Suggested extension: Record and put on YouTube.*<br>Possible points = _____ | **5. Eulogy (Synthesis)**<br>• Follows Oral Presentation criteria card<br>• Focuses on Pericles, Solon, or Cleisthenes<br>• Historically accurate<br>• Tells about the person's life accomplishments and contributions to democratic ideas<br>Possible points = _____ |
| **2. Ballot & Paragraph (Application)**<br>• Ballot has 5 democratic ideas<br>• Organizes class vote and counts votes<br>• Paragraph clearly explains what each of the five results show<br>*Suggested extension: Organize campaign speeches before the vote with people speaking for and against each idea.*<br>Possible points = _____ | **6. Acrostic Poem (Synthesis)**<br>• Poem is 9 lines long, one line for each letter in DEMOCRACY<br>• Accurate information about democratic ideas<br>• Includes history as well as present day<br>*Suggested extension: Memorize your poem and teach it to the class.*<br>Possible points = _____ |
| **3. Venn Diagram (Analysis)**<br>• Follows Venn Diagram criteria card<br>• Shows similarities and differences between Greek and Roman political thought<br>• Includes ideas about how democracy should work<br>*Suggested extension: Compare their ideas to American democratic ideas.*<br>Possible points = _____ | **7. PowerPoint Presentation (Evaluation)**<br>• Follows PowerPoint criteria card<br>• Has an evaluation of how well the Constitution has worked<br>• Has examples for each idea<br>• Uses 3 or more Internet sources in research<br>*Suggested extension: PowerPoint includes important Supreme Court decisions about parts of the Constitution.*<br>Possible points = _____ |
| **4. Oral Presentation (Analysis)**<br>• Follows Oral Presentation criteria card<br>• Explains differences between a dictatorship, constitutional monarchy, and a presidential democracy.<br>• Has examples of each<br>*Suggested extension: Presentation includes relevant visuals.*<br>Possible points = _____ | **8. Chart (Evaluation)**<br>• Follows Chart criteria card<br>• Chart lists 3 criteria of things that would indicate progress toward democracy<br>• Chart rates 5 countries based on this criteria<br>*Suggested extension: Present your chart to the class, and explain your reasons for rating each country the way you did.*<br>Possible points = _____ |

## Individual Lesson Plan™ Scientific Classification/Six Kingdoms

### ACTIVITIES – STUDENT CHOICES

| Linguistic | Kinesthetic |
|---|---|
| 1. Write an **article for a scientific journal or blog** discussing the changes in scientific classification from Aristotle's system to Linnaeus' binomial system to some of the newest classification systems.<br><br>2. Make a **list** of the scientific (Latin) names of 10 species. Find the meaning of each. Then identify 2 or more English words that are derived from each of the Latin terms. | 3. Make **an information cube** with each of the six kingdoms on one side of the cube. Include for each:<br>• Characteristics<br>• Examples<br><br>4. Make a **shadow box** to display and classify 5 varieties of plants growing in your neighborhood. Include a photo, label with name and classification, and a sample in each section. |

| Technological | Visual |
|---|---|
| 5. On your computer, generate a **classification chart** for your favorite wild animal or pet, showing the seven levels of classification from the broadest to the most specific.<br><br>6. Create a **PowerPoint presentation** naming and describing the characteristics of the six kingdoms, including pictures of organisms from each of the kingdoms. | 7. Create a **time line** showing the history of scientific classification from Aristotle to present day techniques.<br><br>8. Create and **draw** your own original species. Then design a **classification chart**, showing the seven levels of classification of this species from the broadest to the most specific. |

| Required Activities<br>Teacher's Choice | Product/Performance<br>Required | Assessment<br>Required Activities |
|---|---|---|
| 1. Do required reading about scientific classification in your science book. Answer required questions. | 1. Answers to questions from Science book. | 1. Accurate answers, all questions completed. |
| 2. Identify 5 "strange groups" of plants and/or animals, and write a short description of the characteristics of each. | 2. Complete taxonomic key for each along with entire class. | 2. Accurate classification of 'strange groups." |
| 3. List at least 20 items found in your kitchen and how they are organized. Write a paragraph comparing this to the seven levels of classification in science. | 3. List and paragraph.<br>*For any student choice activity, include at least 2 resources that support your work. List in correct bibliography form. | 3. Lists 20 items.<br>Explains organization system for the items.<br>Compares organizational system with classifications in science.<br>Paragraph has at least 7 sentences.<br>Neatly written with correct spelling, grammar, and punctuation. |

**Common Core Standards:**
- Make strategic use of digital media and visual displays of data to express information and enhance understanding of presentations.
- Draw evidence from literary or informational texts to support analysis, reflection and research.
- Cite specific textual evidence to support analysis of scientific and technical texts.

| Student Choices in Ways to Learn | Product/Performance<br>Student Choice | Due Dates<br>Student Choice Activities |
|---|---|---|
| Linguistic | | |
| Kinesthetic | | |
| Technological | | |
| Visual | | |

# Assessment of Student Choices - Individual Lesson Plan – Scientific Classification

***Note: For any of the choices below, cite at least two sources to support your work.***

**1. Article for Journal or Blog (Linguistic)**
- Correct grammar, spelling, and punctuation
- Explains at least five changes in scientific classification beginning with Aristotle, including Linnaeus and more recent systems
- Discusses the reasons for these changes
- Correct/accurate information

*Suggested extension: Predict what a new system of classification might be in the future and how it would work.*

Possible points = ______

**3. Information Cube (Kinesthetic)**
- Follows Information Cube criteria card
- Each side has one of the kingdoms
- Describes characteristics of each kingdom
- Has examples of species from each kingdom

*Suggested extension: Make an Information cube showing the 3-Domain system of classification.*

Possible points = ______

**2. List (Linguistic)**
- Has list of Latin names of 10 species
- Correct meaning for each Latin name
- Has 2 or more English words taken from each Latin word

*Suggested extension: Make a crossword puzzle using the 10 Latin names and the 20 English words.*

Possible points = ______

**4. Shadow Box (Kinesthetic)**
- In a sturdy box with five sections
- Has samples of 5 varieties of plants
- Plants are classified correctly
- Includes a photo, name, and label for each

*Suggested extension: Research other locations where each of your 5 plants can be found. Make conclusions about each plant.*

Possible points = ______

**5. Classification Chart (Technological)**
- Follows Chart criteria card – Done on the computer
- Shows the seven levels of classification from broadest to most specific
- Classification accurate for the animal

*Suggested extension: Invent a classification chart for 20 of your favorite videos.*

Possible points = ______

**7. Time Line (Visual)**
- Follows Time Line criteria card
- Shows history of scientific classification in chronological order
- Has at least 6 dates, names, and theories

*Suggested extension: Write a short essay explaining the impact of Charles Darwin's work on scientific classification.*

Possible points = ______

**6. PowerPoint presentation (Technological)**
- Follows PowerPoint criteria card
- Includes names and characteristics of all six kingdoms
- Has 2-3 pictures of organisms from each kingdom

*Suggested extension: Use video footage in the PowerPoint that shows several examples of each kingdom.*

Possible points = ______

**8. Drawing and Classification Chart (Visual)**
- Follows Drawing criteria card
- Follows Chart criteria card
- Drawing clearly shows a new species
- Chart shows each of the 7 levels of classification
- has explanations of why this new species belongs in each

Possible points = ______

# Individual Lesson Plan™ Sea Turtles

## ACTIVITIES – STUDENT CHOICES

| Visual | Written |
|---|---|
| 1. Create a **Venn Diagram** comparing and contrasting sea turtles to komodo dragons.<br><br>2. Create a **Time line** sequencing the life cycle of a sea turtle. Include at least 10 steps. Be specific in the type of sea turtle and its location. | 3. Write a **Persuasive Essay** encouraging others to help save endangered sea turtles. Tell why sea turtles are endangered and at least three things people could do to help this cause.<br><br>4. Find information about a specific type of sea turtle. Write an **Informational Report** about it that is at least 3 paragraphs long. Use at least two sources. |
| **Kinesthetic** | **Technological** |
| 5. Make a **Pop-up book** showing the life cycle of one type of sea turtle. Four different phases of the life cycle should pop up on different pages of your book. Make sure your book includes details about the habitat, the geographical location, and dangers this species may encounter.<br><br>6. Create a **Diorama** showing a specific sea turtle habitat. Be sure to include examples of plant life and other animals the sea turtle might encounter. Present and explain your diorama to the class, telling about this type of sea turtle and what is shown in your diorama. | 7. Create a **PowerPoint Slide Show** showing examples of at least four different sea turtles on four different continents and how they live. Use internet sources for your research.<br><br>8. Using www.seaturtle.org print out a tracking map, and research data to track two sea turtles' travels. Compare and contrast the data between the two turtles using a **Venn Diagram** showing your findings. Include a **Paragraph** on the back of your paper summarizing your findings and your conclusions about the two turtles' travels. |

| Required Activities<br>Teacher's Choice | Product/Performance<br>Required | Assessment<br>Required Activities |
|---|---|---|
| 1. Read text to learn basic information about a sea turtle's life. Answer assigned questions. | 1. Participate in whole class discussions on sea turtles. | 1. Accurate answers to questions and all students participating in class discussions. |
| 2. Define assigned vocabulary words relating to sea turtles and other forms of marine life. | 2. All words correctly defined. | 2. Accurate definitions, all words completed. |
| 3. Write a short story about a group of kids who discover a sea turtle nest. Be scientifically realistic, but use creativity to make your story interesting and exciting. | 3. Short story (2-4 pages) | 3. Story is realistic about the discovery of a sea turtle nest.<br>Story has a beginning, middle, and end.<br>Story has creative elements.<br>Correct writing conventions.<br>Clear and coherent writing. |

**Common Core Standards:**
- Read and comprehend complex literary and informational texts independently and proficiently.
- Make strategic use of digital media and visual displays of data to express information and enhance understanding of presentations.
- Acquire and use accurately a range of general academic and domain specific words and phrases
- Produce clear and coherent writing in which the development, organization and style are appropriate to task, purpose and audience.

| Student Choices in Ways to Learn | Product/Performance<br>Student Choice | Due Dates<br>Student Choice Activities |
|---|---|---|
| Visual | | |
| Written | | |
| Kinesthetic | | |
| Technological | | |

# Assessment of Student Choices - Individual Lesson Plan - Sea Turtles

**1. Venn Diagram (Visual)**
- Follows Venn Diagram criteria card
- Compares/contrasts sea turtles and komodo dragons
- Has at least 3 similarities and differences
- Correct information

*Suggested extension: Compares a third sea reptile with these two and shows in written or visual form.*

Possible points = ______

**2. Time Line (Visual)**
- Follows Time Line criteria card
- Shows correct sequence of life cycle
- Includes 10 steps
- Specifies type and location of sea turtle

*Suggested extension: Notes portions of the life cycle that are the most dangerous for this sea turtle.*

Possible points = ______

**3. Persuasive Essay (Written)**
- Gives reasons to help endangered sea turtles
- Explains why sea turtles are endangered
- Tells 3 things reader could do to help the cause
- Clear and coherent writing with good organization and planning

*Suggested extension: Speaks to class, a group of parents, or another group of kids or adults sharing the ideas in the essay.*

Possible points = ______

**4. Informational Report (Written)**
- At least 3 paragraphs long
- Accurate information about a specific sea turtle
- Lists two or more sources
- Clear and coherent writing with good organization and planning

*Suggested extension: Creates some type of visual (map, chart, etc.) to go with the report.*

Possible points = ______

**5. Pop-up Book (Kinesthetic)**
- Follows Pop-up Book criteria card
- Shows life cycle of one type of sea turtle
- Includes details about habitat, geography, and dangers
- At least 4 pop-ups

*Suggested extension: Read story to younger students at a lower grade level.*

Possible points = ______

**6. Diorama (Kinesthetic)**
- Follows Diorama criteria card
- Follows Oral Presentation criteria card
- Habitat accurate for the type of sea turtle shown
- Has several examples of plants and other animals in the habitat

*Suggested extension: Explains relationships between different animals in the habitat within a food chain or web.*

Possible points = ______

**7. PowerPoint Presentation (Technological)**
- Follows PowerPoint criteria card
- Has examples of 4 different sea turtles on 4 different continents
- Explains how these sea turtles live
- Uses 3 or more Internet sources in research

*Suggested extension: PowerPoint includes appropriate short video clips of these turtles.*

Possible points = ______

**8. Venn Diagram & Paragraph (Technological)**
- Uses web site to find information and track two sea turtles
- Has a Venn Diagram to compare and contrast data
- Paragraph is a concise and accurate summary of findings and conclusion

*Suggested extension: Email several people who live near the turtles' habitats and ask for more information about your turtles.*

Possible points = ______

## Individual Lesson Plan™ Statistics & Probability

### ACTIVITIES – STUDENT CHOICES.

| Application | Synthesis |
|---|---|
| 1. Toss 10 coins 120 times or more. Record the number of heads for each tossing. Make a **plot of frequency polygon**. Find the mean and standard deviation for this group of data.<br><br>2. Collect final test scores from 100 students. Make a **score-frequency plot**. Find the mean and standard deviation. | 5. Search the Internet to find the failure rate of a new product. Write an **article** recommending or rejecting this product by using a statistical analysis.<br><br>6. Use statistics to analyze the test results at your school in a given subject. Using these statistics, identify the strongest and weakest areas. Write a **letter** to the superintendent suggesting ways to improve. |
| **Analysis** | **Evaluation** |
| 3. **Toss a coin** 10 times, and find the probability of 1 heads up to 10 heads up. Compare and contrast with the plot of frequency polygon.<br><br>4. Design or use an existing computer program to **analyze the test results** for students at your school. Find the mean and standard deviation. Write at least three conclusions you can make from this data. | 7. Write a **blog** to explain the importance of statistics in scientific research. Explain how statistics can sometimes be used incorrectly thereby generating faulty conclusions.<br><br>8. Research three different error analysis techniques. Make a **chart** showing the advantages and disadvantages of each. Write a paragraph explaining which one you think is best and why. |

| Required Activities Teacher's Choice | Product/Performance Required | Assessment Required Activities |
|---|---|---|
| 1. Read each section of your math book chapter on probability and statistics. Write all formulas with parameters in your notes. | 1. Written formulas with parameters in notes. | 1. Accurate formulas.<br>All formulas are done. |
| 2. In a group, make posters to show mean, median, mode, and whisker-box plot. | 2. One or more posters. | 2. Follows Poster criteria card.<br>Shows mean, median, mode, and whisker-box plot.<br>Done in a group. |
| 3. With a partner, show a real life example of Normal Distribution and Standard Deviation. | 3. Demonstration or oral report with visual. | 3. Shows a real life example of Normal Distribution and Standard Deviation.<br>Logical and clear explanation.<br>Correct and accurate. |

**Common Core Standards:**
- Summarize, represent and interpret data on a single count or measurement variable
- Calculate expected values and use them to solve problems.
- Use probability to evaluate outcomes of decisions.

| Student Choices in Ways to Learn | Product/Performance Student Choice | Due Dates Student Choice Activities |
|---|---|---|
| Application | | |
| Analysis | | |
| Synthesis | | |
| Evaluation | | |

## Assessment of Student Choices - Individual Lesson Plan – Statistics & Probability

**1. Plot of Frequency Polygon (Application)**
- Has a plot of frequency polygon
- Records at least 120 coin tosses
- Uses 10 coins
- Accurate mean and standard deviation

*Suggested extension: Compare results with other students doing the same thing and make conclusions based on their results and yours.*

Possible points = ______

**2. Score-Frequency Plot (Application)**
- Has test scores from 100 students
- Has an accurate score-frequency plot based on these scores
- Accurate mean and standard deviation

*Suggested extension: Do the same thing with test scores from a different group of students: another grade level, an honors class, a remedial class, etc. What conclusions can you make?*

Possible points = ______

**3. Coin Toss (Analysis)**
- Has the probability of 1 head up to 10 heads up
- Compares and contrasts with the results someone got doing Student Choice Activity 1
- Writes at least three conclusions

*Suggested extension: Repeat several times and compare and contrast your results.*

Possible points = ______

**4. Test Analysis using a Computer (Analysis)**
- Uses selected computer program correctly
- Enters data accurately
- Correct mean and standard deviation
- Has three or more logical conclusions based on the data

Possible points = ______

**5. Written article (Synthesis)**
- Does research using an appropriate search engine, finds and records failure rate of a new product
- Correct statistical analysis
- Correct grammar, punctuation, and spelling
- Clear and coherent writing stating point of view

*Suggested extension: Post article on the Internet and ask for comments.*

Possible points = ______

**6. Letter using Statistics (Synthesis)**
- Uses correct letter format
- Correct grammar, punctuation, and spelling
- Weakest and strongest areas identified using statistics
- Suggests ways to improve

*Suggested extension: Make an appointment and meet with the superintendent to discuss your ideas.*

Possible points = ______

**7. Blog (Evaluation)**
- Follows Blog criteria card
- Explains importance of statistics in scientific research
- Gives examples of the faulty use of statistics in scientific research

*Suggested extension: Debate someone with another point of view. Use statistics correctly to state your position in this debate.*

Possible points = ______

**8. Chart & Paragraph (Evaluation)**
- Follows Chart criteria card
- Evidence of research on three different error analysis techniques
- Chart shows advantages and disadvantages of each type of error analysis technique
- Paragraph clearly explains which technique you think is the best and why

Possible points = ______

# Individual Lesson Plan™ Using the Internet

## ACTIVITIES – STUDENT CHOICES

| Visual | Verbal |
|---|---|
| 1. Visit any web site to get an idea of how it is designed. Print out five or more pages. Then **label the parts** of this web site. Include menus, graphics, links, text, URL, pictures, contact information, and a search box.<br><br>2. Use your own knowledge, a search engine, or your text-book, and list at least 20 Internet-related words. Define each. Then make a **crossword** puzzle using all of the words. Provide an answer key. | **5. Interview** 3 different people who use the Internet in their jobs and personal lives. Include 5 or more questions to find out this information. Write a summary of what you learned from these interviews.<br><br>6. Write **two paragraphs** about how you use or could use the Internet. What can you accomplish online that would otherwise take more time, effort, or resources? Be specific. |
| **Kinesthetic** | **Technological** |
| 3. With a partner, write and present a **skit** showing at least 10 things you shouldn't do when using the Internet. Create a poster with your Top Ten to display in your classroom.<br><br>4. Make a set of 10 **flash cards** that would teach kindergarten or first graders some basic terminology about the Internet and how it works. Have the word on the front and a picture or diagram on the back. Share these with at least one child who is seven years old or younger. | 7. Visit six different web sites, each ending in a different set of letters. For example, gov, net, mil, com, org, and edu. Research about each. Then make a **list** telling what type of site it is and a **summary** of each. Post on your class web site or send the information to your teacher as an email attachment.<br><br>8. Write a **blog** of at least two paragraphs, one about the advantages of having a global community connected by the Internet and the other about the disadvantages. Post on your school or class web site. |

| Required Activities Teacher's Choice | Product/Performance Required | Assessment Required Activities |
|---|---|---|
| 1. As a class, discuss the value of the Internet. On the board, list ways to use the Internet. | 1. Class list on the board. | 1. Accurate and complete list. All participate. |
| 2. Discuss as a class why some ideas and information found on the Internet might not be true. In partners, go to the Internet and find 5 statements. Then find 5 other statements that contradict the first 5 statements. Write them down with web site references. | 2. Lists with a total of 10 statements from the Internet. | 2. Lists of 5 statements and 5 contradictory statements.<br>All statements are from the Internet.<br>Websites are cited for each. |
| 3. Each student will select four of his/her classes. For each class, write a paragraph about how you could use the Internet in that class. | 3. Four paragraphs about how the Internet can be used in four classes. | 3. Has a total of 4 paragraphs.<br>Each paragraph highlights a different class.<br>Each paragraph tells how the Internet can be used in each class. |

**Common Core Standards:**
- Integrate and evaluate content presented in diverse formats and media, including visually and quantitatively as well as in words.
- Use technology, including the Internet, to produce and publish writing and to interact and collaborate with others.

| Student Choices in Ways to Learn | Product/Performance Student Choice | Due Dates Student Choice Activities |
|---|---|---|
| **Visual** | | |
| **Verbal** | | |
| **Kinesthetic** | | |
| **Technological** | | |

# Assessment of Student Choices - Individual Lesson Plan – Using the Internet

**1. Labeled Website Pages (Visual)**
- Website address clearly shown____
- Five or more pages are printed out.____
- Labels include Menus, Graphics. Links, Text, URL, Pictures and a Search box.____
- Each page is labeled____

*Suggested extension: Write an evaluation of the effectiveness of this website design, including what you liked and what you would improve.*

Possible points = ______

**2. Crossword Puzzle (Visual)**
- Follows Crossword Puzzle criteria card____
- Answer key is provided____
- Across and Down definitions are accurate____
- Has 20 Internet-related words

*Suggested extension: Use words and abbreviations that have an Internet meaning and another meaning.*

Possible points = ______

**3. Skit (Kinesthetic)**
- Follows Skit criteria card____
- Clearly shows 10 things you shouldn't do when using the Internet____
- Poster lists the Top Ten things ____

*Suggested extension: Have someone video your skit and post it on YouTube.*

Possible points = ______

**4. Flash Cards (Kinesthetic)**
- Uses index cards, cardboard or tag board ____
- Has 10 flash cards____
- Has word on one side and picture or diagram on the other____
- Terminology is related to the Internet____
- Shares flash cards with at least one child ____

Possible points = ______

**5. Interview (Verbal)**
- Interviews 3 different people____
- Has 5 or more questions to ask each person____
- Written summary explains what was learned____

*Suggested extension: Develop a Venn Diagram that shows what you learned about advantages and disadvantages of the Internet from those you interviewed.*

Possible points = ______

**6. Paragraphs (Verbal)**
- Has two paragraphs____
- Correct spelling, grammar, and punctuation____
- Includes four or more different uses for the Internet____
- Accurate information____
- Specific information____

Possible points = ______

**7. List and Summary (Technological)**
- Visited six different types of web sites____
- List has type of site and summary for each____
- Information is posted or shared technologically____
- Accurate research and information____
- Correct spelling, grammar, punctuation____

Possible points = ______

**8. Blog (Technological)**
- Follows Blog criteria card____
- Has at least two paragraphs____
- One paragraph is about advantages of global connectivity and the other is about disadvantages____
- Accurate ____
- Correct spelling, grammar, punctuation____

Possible points = ______

# Individual Lesson Plan™ Volcanoes

## ACTIVITIES – STUDENT CHOICES

| Visual | Verbal |
|---|---|
| 1. Draw a **diagram** showing the internal parts of a volcano. Include information in your diagram showing how volcanoes erupt.<br><br>2. On a world **map**, show the location of at least 10 major volcanoes. Label each along with the date of their last eruption. | 5. Write a **poem** responding to a character or incident in the fiction story you read.<br><br>6. Choose a well-known volcano. Write a **folk tale** explaining why it erupted. |
| **Kinesthetic** | **Technological** |
| 3. Make an **information cube** about volcanoes. You can choose 6 different volcanoes, one for each side of the cube, or you can choose six characteristics, interesting facts, and information about volcanoes to include on your cube.<br><br>4. Make a two-sided **diorama** that shows a location before a volcano erupts and after it erupts. This should be a real volcano, so research your location carefully. Make an index card telling the location, volcano's name, and other important facts. | 7. Log on to www.volcanoes.com. You will find a wealth of information and links to other sites. Explore this site and its links, and write down 10 new things that you learn about volcanoes. Indicate the web site address for each.<br><br>8. Do an **Internet search** of children's fiction books about volcanoes. Read summaries of 3 different books, and decide which you would like to read. Write the titles of all three books and a sentence about each. Then **write** why you chose the one you did. |

| Required Activities Teacher's Choice | Product/Performance Required | Assessment Required Activities |
|---|---|---|
| 1. Read a fiction and a non-fiction book about volcanoes. These can be selected by the teacher or by the student. Discuss each. | 1. Contribute to discussion. | 1. Informal observations during class discussion. |
| 2. Create a story map of the fiction story. | 2. Story map. | 2. Correct story map with at least 5 events listed in order. |
| 3. Make a list of 10 important facts about volcanoes that you learned from the non-fiction book. | 3. List. | 3. List has 10 important facts about volcanoes. Accuracy. |

**Common Core Standards:**

- Produce clear and coherent writing in which the development, organization and style are appropriate to task, purpose and audience.
- Integrate and evaluate content presented in diverse formats and media, including visually and quantitatively as well as in words.

| Student Choices in Ways to Learn | Product/Performance Student Choice | Due Dates Student Choice Activities |
|---|---|---|
| Visual | | |
| Verbal | | |
| Kinesthetic | | |
| Technological | | |

## Assessment of Student Choices - Individual Lesson Plan – Volcanoes

**1. Diagram (Visual)**
- Follows Diagram criteria card____
- Shows at least 6 parts of a volcano____
- Has information about how volcanoes erupt____
- Volcano parts are labeled____

*Suggested extension: Research three different volcanoes to see if there are different types of eruptions.*

Possible points = ______

**2. Map Locations (Visual)**
- Uses a world map____
- Shows locations of 10 volcanoes on the map____
- Name of each volcano and date of last eruption are on labels____

*Suggested extension: Include additional volcanoes along with reasons why each erupted when it did.*

Possible points = ______

**3. Information Cube (Kinesthetic)**
- Follows Information Cube criteria card____
- Cube either has information about 6 different volcanoes or 6 characteristics and information about one volcano____

*Suggested extension: Cube includes little-known volcanoes and/or little-known facts that required extensive research.*

Possible points = ______

**4. Diorama (Kinesthetic)**
- Follows Diorama criteria card ____
- Diorama has two sides or sections ____
- One side shows location before eruption____
- Other side shows same location after eruption____
- Index card has location, volcano's name, and basic facts ____

Possible points = ______

**5. Poem (Verbal)**
- Follows Poem criteria card____
- Poem responds to a character or incident in the story____
- Uses descriptive words____

*Suggested extension: Make your poem a narrative poem and add a new ending to the story you read.*

Possible points = ______

**6. Folk Tale (Verbal)**
- Has a beginning, middle, and end____
- Correct spelling, grammar, and punctuation____
- Tells a story that involves a volcano____
- Folktale explains in an imaginary way why the volcano erupted____

Possible points = ______

**7. List of New Things Learned (Technological)**
- Visited www.volcanoes.com and looked at the information____
- Has a list with 10 new things that were learned____
- Web site addresses given for each item on the list____

*Suggested extension: Evaluate several web sites that focus on volcanoes. Which do you think are the best and why?*

Possible points = ______

**8. Internet Search (Technological)**
- Search includes at least 5 different web sites____
- Has titles of 3 different fiction books about volcanoes ____
- Has a sentence about each book____
- Writes why one book was chosen ____
- Correct spelling, grammar, punctuation____

Possible points = ______

# Individual Lesson Plan™ ____________________

ACTIVITIES – STUDENT CHOICES

| Choice Category #1 | Choice Category #2 |
| --- | --- |
| | |

| Choice Category #3 | Choice Category #4 |
| --- | --- |
| | |

| Required Activities<br>Teacher's Choice | Product/Performance<br>Required | Assessment<br>Required Activities |
| --- | --- | --- |
| | | |

Common Core Standards:

| Student Choices in Ways to Learn | Product/Performance<br>Student Choice | Due Dates<br>Student Choice Activities |
| --- | --- | --- |
| Choice Category #1 | | |
| Choice Category #2 | | |
| Choice Category #3 | | |
| Choice Category #4 | | |

## Assessment of Student Choices - Individual Lesson Plan

______________________

**1.**

•
•
•
•

Possible points = ______

**2.**

•
•
•
•

Possible points = ______

**3.**

•
•
•
•

Possible points = ______

**4.**

•
•
•
•

Possible points = ______

**5.**

•
•
•
•

Possible points = ______

**6.**

•
•
•
•

Possible points = ______

**7.**

•
•
•
•

Possible points = ______

**8.**

•
•
•
•

Possible points = ______

# Primary Individual Lesson Plan (ILP™)

## THE PRIMARY INDIVIDUAL LESSON PLAN (ILP™)

The original Individual Lesson Plan™ format was for students in grades 3-9. I soon realized the student choice activities were both appropriate and valuable for even younger students. Those students, however, might have great difficulty trying to navigate and understand the ILP™ format. For these reasons, I created a simpler version of the form called the Primary ILP™.

The Primary ILP™ has all of the elements of the more complex version. It includes:

- Title
- Common Core Standards
- Required Activity (at the teacher's discretion)
- Four squares that can hold up to eight Student Choice Activities

When introducing this format to young children, start with only four Student Choice Activities. As they become more familiar with making choices and doing this type of differentiation, increase the number of choices to eight. Sometimes each choice takes only a few minutes, and sometimes it may take a day or two. However, the choices are never as complex and time-consuming as they are for older students.

One important thing to keep in mind is that you cannot give students choices to make products or do performances if they have never been introduced to them and don't know how to do them. With younger children, you first have to build their capacity for doing independent work and completing projects/products before you can offer these as choices.

Give students the Primary ILP™ form, and have them circle their choices. At other times put the choices on the bulletin board, and have each student put a sticky note on the one he or she wants to do. You may want to add pictures to illustrate the choices as is done on the 100s Day Primary ILP™.

Primary Individual Lesson Plans (ILP™) with corresponding assessments include:



At the end of this section is a blank form entitled ILP™ for Primary Students and a blank Primary ILP™ Assessment form to use as you write your own ILPs™.

# Primary ILP™ - Title of Lesson: 100s Day

**Math Domain: Counting and Cardinality**
**Math Domain: Measurement and Data**

**Common Core Standards:**

- Count to 100 by ones and tens.
- Classify objects into given categories; count the number of objects in each category and sort the categories by count.

## Visual

1. **Touch Count** to 100 using a hundreds chart.

| 1 | 2 | 3 | 4 | 5 |
|---|---|---|---|---|
| 6 | 7 | 8 | 8 | 10 |
| 11 | 12 | 13 | 14 | 15 |
| 16 | 17 | 18 | 19 | 20 |

2. Find **pictures in magazines** that show 5s, 10s or 100s. Cut them out and paste on construction paper. Label each with the correct number.

## Kinesthetic

3. Create a 100s **Fruit Loop Necklace** grouping colors by 1, 5 or 10s. The total number of Fruit Loops used should equal 100.

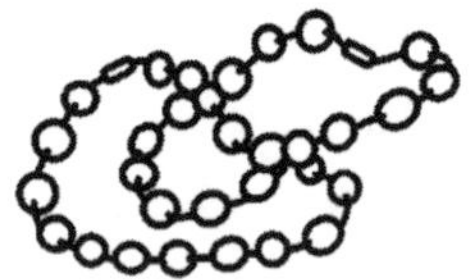

4. Glue (gems, beads, stickers) into strips or rows of 10 to create a 100s **Crown.**

## Technological

5. Count to 100 playing **Snakes and Ladders** on the computer.

6. Search on the **Internet** for three **websites** that show 100. Print out information you find.

## Auditory/Verbal

7. **Write or tell a story** about the number 100.

8. **Sing a Song** about the number 100.

## Primary ILP™ Assessment: 100s Day

### Visual

**1. Touch Counting**
- Accurate counting up to 100
- Touches correct numbers as they are said orally.

*Extension: Writes numbers 1-100 in correct order on a grid or chart*

**2. Pictures in Magazines**
- Pictures show 5, 10, and 100
- Pictures are labeled with correct numbers
- Cutting and pasting shows neatness and care

*Extension: Shows addition and/or subtraction of these numbers through these pictures.*

### Kinesthetic

**3. Fruit Loop Necklace**
- Colors are grouped by 1, 5 and 10s
- Used a total of 100 Fruit Loops

*Extension: Has an unusual or unique pattern in the placement of the Fruit Loops that can logically be explained by the student.*

**4. Crown**
- Has 10 rows with 10 items in each row

*Extension: Has an unusual or unique pattern in the placement of the items that can logically be explained by the student.*

### Technological

**5. Snakes and Ladders**
- Follows rules of the game
- Accurate counting to 100

*Extension: Can count to 120 or more.*

**6. Web site Search**
- Has three different web sites
- Each web site shows 100
- Information is printed out.

*Extension: Use the 'Contact Us' button and email the web site, telling them something more you know about 100.*

### Auditory/Verbal

**7. Story**
- Story is about 100
- Story has a beginning, middle, and end
- Easy to follow and understand

*Extension: Story includes some other numbers or number combinations.*

**8. Song**
- Song is about 100
- Has at least 4 lines
- We could hear you sing

*Extension: Song includes other numbers or number combinations.*

# Primary ILP™ - Title: Fact and Fiction in Books

**Anchor Standard: LA/Reading: Key Ideas and Details**
**Anchor Standard: LA/Reading: Literature: Craft and Structure**

**Common Core Standards:**

- Read closely to determine what the text says explicitly and to make logical inferences from it; cite specific textual evidence when writing or speaking to support conclusions drawn from the text.
- Explain major differences between books that tell stories and books that give information.

**Required:** All students will read (or have read to them) a fairy tale and an informational text. The subject of the two should be linked in some way; for example, Cinderella and a book about castles.

| Visual | Kinesthetic |
|---|---|
| **1. Drawings**<br><br>Draw three things found in the fairy tale that are real. Explain why you think they are real. | **2. Skit**<br><br>Act out a part of the fairy tale that shows it is not real. Include the setting as well as words and actions. Explain why this shows the story is not real. |
| **Technological** | **Auditory/Verbal** |
| **3. Internet Facts**<br><br>Look on the Internet and find out three more facts about the topic of your true story. Write them on the computer, and print them out. | **4. Oral presentation**<br><br>Do an oral presentation explaining three differences between a true story and a fantasy story. Give examples from the two books you read. |

## Primary ILP™ Assessment: Fact and Fiction in Books

| Visual | Kinesthetic |
|---|---|
| **1. Drawings**<br>• Draws three real things from the fairy tale<br>• Accurate explanation of why they are real<br>• Follows Drawing criteria card<br><br>*Extension: Includes text from the fairy tale with the drawing and evidence from the real world that these things could be true.* | **2. Skit**<br>• Skit has both actions and words<br>• Setting explained or indicated through props and scenery<br>• Accurate explanation of why this part of the fairy tale is not real<br><br>*Extension: Compares this fairy tale to another fairy tale that also has parts that are not real.* |
| **Technological** | **Auditory/Verbal** |
| **3. Internet Facts**<br>• Facts are different from the facts learned from reading the true story<br>• Facts relate to the topic<br>• Written in complete sentences<br>• Printed from the computer<br><br>*Extension: Find facts about parts of the fairy tale that show some of it could be true.* | **4. Oral Presentation**<br>• Follows Oral Presentation criteria card<br>• Accurately explains 3 differences between a true story and a fantasy story<br>• Gives examples from the books read<br><br>*Extension: Has a visual aid to use with the presentation.* |

# Primary ILP™ - Title: Measurement

**Math Domain: Measurement and Data**

**Common Core Standards:**

- Measure the length of an object by selecting and using appropriate tools such as rulers, yardsticks, meter sticks and measuring tapes.
- Estimate lengths using units of inches, feet, centimeters and meters.

**Required:**

As a whole class activity, introduce the students to a number of measurement tools and have them practice using them. Using objects found in the classroom, have students estimate their lengths in inches, feet, centimeters and meters.
Each student will choose two of the activities listed below and will do them with a partner.

| **1. Estimating and Measuring Objects**<br><br>With a partner, estimate the length in inches of each of five objects given to you by the teacher. Then use a ruler and measure to the nearest ¼ inch. Write a sentence explaining how close your estimate was. | **2. Measuring Your Body**<br><br>With a partner, measure these body parts in inches and centimeters. Write down the measurements for you and for your partner.<br><br>• Thumb<br>• Arm from elbow to wrist<br>• Foot<br>• Longest fingernail<br><br>Then measure your height using feet and meters. |
|---|---|
| **3. Measuring School Spaces**<br><br>Estimate the length in both feet and meters of the following:<br><br>• Whiteboard or Smart Board<br>• Classroom wall<br>• Distance between the door of your classroom to the door of the lunchroom<br>• Top of your teacher's desk<br><br>Then use a ruler, yardstick, and a meter stick and do actual measurements in feet and meters. Write what you learned. | **4. Using Tape Measurements**<br><br>With a partner, use a measuring tape to measure the following in both inches and centimeters:<br><br>• Around your wrist<br>• Around your waist<br>• Around a jar or can<br>• Around your head<br><br>Write down your measurements for each with two sentences explaining when and why you should use a measuring tape rather than a ruler. |

# Primary ILP™ Assessment: Measurement

## 1. Estimating and Measuring Objects

- Has estimates of the length in inches of 5 objects
- Uses ruler to measure each to nearest ¼ inch
- Name of object, estimate, and actual measurement written clearly
- Has a sentence explaining how close the estimate was

*Extension: Estimates lengths in feet, yards or meters of larger objects and measures them.*

## 2. Measuring Your Body

- Measurements are in inches and centimeters
- Has measurements for thumb, arm from elbow to wrist, foot, and fingernail
- Has measurement for height in feet and meters
- Has measurements for both people

*Extension: Measure the length of hair of the person with the longest hair in your class and the shortest hair in your class. Make sure you have their permission first!*

## 3. Measuring School Spaces

- Length is estimated in both feet and meters
- Includes whiteboard or Smart Board, wall, classroom to lunchroom, teacher's desk
- Has actual measurements of the above in both feet and meters
- Has written explanation of what was learned

*Extension: Estimate and measure other classroom and school spaces. Make sure you have permission if you need to leave the classroom to do this.*

## 4. Using Tape Measurements

- Measurements are done with a tape measure
- Measurements are in inches and centimeters
- Has measurements for wrist, waist, jar or can, and head
- Has two sentences about when and why you need to use tape measures

*Extension: Estimate and then measure other objects that are best measured with a tape measure. Write down your results. Why is it more difficult to estimate results when you use a tape measure?*

# Primary ILP™ - Title of Lesson: Long and Short Vowel Sounds

**Anchor Standard: LA/Reading: Foundational Skills**
**Anchor Standard: LA/Writing: Text Types and Purpose**

**Common Core Standards:**

- Distinguish long from short vowel sounds in spoken single-syllable words.
- Distinguish long and short vowels when reading one-syllable words.
- Write narratives that recount two or more sequenced events.
- Write opinion pieces that state an opinion and a reason for the opinion.

| Visual | Kinesthetic |
|---|---|
| **1. Picture Cards**<br>Use picture cards to identify the picture and the short vowel sound or the long vowel sound in the word. Place the card on the vowel sound chart under the correct vowel sound.<br><br>**2. Story**<br>Select a story and find 10 words with short vowel sounds. Write each word on a piece of paper and write the short vowel sound each one has. | **3. Making Words with Letter Cards**<br>Use letter cards to create 10 different words, one word for each short vowel sound and one for each long vowel sound.<br><br>**4. Textured Letter Cards**<br>Use textured letter cards to create 5 words with short vowel sounds and 5 words with long vowel sounds. Read each word, and trace each word with your finger. |
| **Writing** | **Auditory/Verbal** |
| **5. Sentences**<br>Write 5 sentences that tell about something that happened to you. Find one word in each sentence with a short vowel sound and one with a long vowel sound. Circle the short vowels and underline the long vowels.<br><br>**6. Book Review**<br>Write sentences stating your opinion about a book or story you have read. Find at least 3 long vowels and 3 short vowels in the words you have written. Circle the short vowels and underline the long vowels. | **7. Sing a Song** Students will learn and sing a song that focuses on the short vowel sounds.<br><br>**8. Recite a Poem:** Students will recite a poem that focuses on long vowel sounds. Each long vowel sound needs to be emphasized as they recite the poem. |

## Primary ILP™ Assessment: Short and Long Vowel Sounds

| Visual | Kinesthetic |
| --- | --- |
| **1. Picture Cards**<br>• Identifies the picture correctly<br>• Identifies short vowels in the word<br>• Identifies long vowels in the word<br>• Correct placement on chart<br><br>**2. Story**<br>• Identifies 10 words with short vowel sounds<br>• Writes each word correctly<br>• Correctly writes the short vowel sound for each word<br><br>*Extension: Identifies and writes 10 long vowel sounds from words in the story.* | **3. Making Words with Letter Cards**<br>• Created 10 different words<br>• All short and long vowel sounds are used in the 10 words<br><br>*Extension: Has words with both short and long vowel sounds in the same word.*<br><br>**4. Textured Letter Cards**<br>• Has 5 words with short vowel sounds<br>• Has 5 words with long vowel sounds<br>• Words read aloud correctly |
| **Writing** | **Auditory/Verbal** |
| **5. Sentences**<br>• Writes 5 sentences<br>• Sentences tell about what happened to the student<br>• Long and short vowel sounds correctly identified in each sentence<br><br>**6. Book Review**<br>• Sentences state an opinion<br>• 3 long vowels and 3 short vowels correctly identified<br><br>*Extension: Compare and contrast your opinion of two stories.* | **7. Song**<br>• Song has lots of words with short vowel sounds<br>• Student can identify the short vowel sounds in the words<br><br>*Extension: Student makes up a song about short vowel sounds.*<br><br>**8. Poem**<br>• Poem has lots of long vowel sounds<br>• Long vowel sounds are emphasized as poem is said |

# Primary ILP™ - Title of Lesson: Solar System

**Anchor Standard: LA/Reading: Range of Reading and Level of Text Complexity**

**Common Core Standards:**

- Use illustrations and details in a text to describe its key ideas.
- Read and comprehend informational texts, including history/social studies, science and technical texts.

**Required Activity:**

- All students will read (or have read to them) an informational picture book or text on the Solar System.
- The entire class will discuss what they know about the Solar System and what they learned from the book that they didn't know before.

| Visual | Mathematical/Logical |
|---|---|
| **1. Drawing of Earth**<br>Pretend you are an astronaut looking at Earth from outer space. Draw a picture of what you see. Be as accurate as you can.<br><br>**2. Drawing of a new Planet**<br>Create a new planet in our solar system. Draw a diagram of where its location would be, and write a paragraph describing what your new planet is like. | **3. Bar Graph**<br>Find out the diameter of the eight planets. Create a bar graph that shows this information.<br><br>**4. Venn Diagram**<br>Use a Venn Diagram to compare and contrast a planet and a star. |
| **Kinesthetic** | **Verbal** |
| **5. Model**<br>Create a model of the sun. Label at least 6 parts of the sun.<br><br>**6. Board Game**<br>Make a board game or card game about the solar system. Play your game with a friend. | **7. Oral Report**<br>Find out about 4 objects in our night sky besides planets. Report on each and include a picture to show the location of each.<br><br>**8. Reading a Story**<br>Read a story about the solar system. Share three of your favorite parts by reading them to your class. |

# Primary ILP™ Assessment: Solar System

## Visual

**1. Drawing of Earth**
- Follows Drawing criteria card
- Is a drawing of Earth
- Earth is the correct shape
- Shows a view of continents and oceans

**2. Drawing of a new Planet**
- Shows diagram of solar system with new planet in it
- Describes new planet's landforms, water, temperature, and other details

## Mathematical/Logical

**3. Bar Graph**
- Accurate diameters for planets
- Includes all eight planets
- Bar graph neat with numbers indicated for diameters

**4. Venn Diagram**
- Follows Venn Diagram criteria card
- Clearly shows 3 or more differences between a planet and a star

## Kinesthetic

**5. Model**
- Has a model of the sun
- Labels show 6 or more parts
- Accurate

**6. Board Game**
- Game is about the solar system
- Game helps teach at least 10 facts about the solar system
- Neatly made

*Suggested extension: Play your game with a friend.*

## Verbal

**7. Oral Report**
- Tells about 4 objects in the sky other than the planets
- Has a picture showing the location of each

*Extension: Tell how each object got in the sky.*

**8. Reading a Story**
- Story is about the solar system
- Picks three different parts
- Reading is clear, loud enough, and expressive

# Primary ILP™ - Title of Lesson: Spiders

**Anchor Standard: LA/Reading: Informational Text: Key Ideas and Details**
**Anchor Standard: LA/Writing: Research to Build and Present Knowledge**
**Anchor Standard: LA/Reading: Integration of Knowledge and Ideas**
**Anchor Standard: LA/Writing: Text Types and Purpose**

**Common Core Standards:**

- Identify the main topic and retell key details in a text.
- Recall information from experiences or gather information from provided sources to answer a question.
- Use illustrations and details in a text to describe its key ideas.
- Write informative/explanatory texts in which they name a topic, supply some facts about the topic and provide some sense of closure.

| Visual | Vocabulary |
|---|---|
| **1. Comic Strip**<br>Draw a comic strip that shows how spiders catch insects in their web. Make sure you show the correct sequence.<br><br>**2. Drawing using Markers**<br>Draw a spider with the correct number of body parts and the correct number of legs. Show fangs and a face. Draw with a pencil first and then use the markers. | **5. List with Definitions**<br>List 10 words that have to do with spiders. Define each word.<br><br>**6. Types of Spider Webs**<br>• Define and illustrate each of these:<br>• Cob web<br>• Sheet web<br>• Funnel web<br>• Orb web |
| **• Writing** | **Poems and Songs** |
| **3. Letter**<br>Write a letter to Anansi the Spider or Charlotte the Spider (both are well-known book characters) explaining what it is like to be a good friend. Tell Anansi or Charlotte why he/she is or isn't a good friend.<br><br>**4. Short Story**<br>Write a short story about a spider. Your story should have dialogue (talking) between the spider and at least one other character. | **7. Song**<br>Write a factual song about spiders that can be sung to the tune of "The Itsy-Bitsy Spider." Your song should have at least 4 facts about spiders.<br><br>**8. Poem**<br>Write a poem about spiders that has at least 6 lines. Use rhyming words in your poem. |

## Primary ILP™ Assessment: Spiders

| Visual | Vocabulary |
| --- | --- |
| **1. Comic Strip**<br>• Follows Comic Strip criteria card<br>• Shows sequence of how a spider catches insects in his web<br>• Accurate<br><br>**2. Drawing using Markers**<br>• Follows Drawing criteria card<br>• Has the correct number of body parts and correct number of legs<br>• Has fangs and a face<br><br>*Extension: Drawing shows spider in a web.* | **3. List with Definitions**<br>• Has 10 words related to spiders<br>• Has definitions for each word<br><br>*Extension: Make an illustrated dictionary using these words.*<br><br>**4. Types of Spider Webs**<br>• Defines all four types of spider webs<br>• Has pictures of all four<br>• Accurate<br><br>*Extension: Explains why different spiders have different kinds of webs.* |
| **Writing** | **Poems and Songs** |
| **5. Letter**<br>• Correct letter format<br>• Letter is to Anansi or Charlotte<br>• Explains what a good friend is<br>• Says why Anansi or Charlotte are or are not good friends<br><br>**6. Short Story**<br>• Story is about a spider<br>• Has a beginning, middle, and end<br>• Has characters and dialogue<br><br>*Extension: Illustrate your story.* | **7. Song**<br>• Follows Song criteria card<br>• Song has at least 4 facts about spiders<br>• Can be sung to the tune "The Itsy-Bitsy Spider"<br><br>*Extension: Sing your song to the class.*<br><br>**8. Poem**<br>• Poem has at least 6 lines<br>• Poem is about spiders<br>• Has rhyming words<br><br>*Extension: Recite your poem for the class.* |

# Primary ILP™

**Title of Lesson:**

**Standards:**

**Required Activities:**

| Category 1 | Category 2 |
|---|---|
| **Category 3** | **Category 4** |

## Primary ILP™ Assessment: ______________________

| Category 1 | Category 2 |
| --- | --- |
| Category 3 | Category 4 |

# QUESTIVITIES™

## QUESTIVITIES™

Questivities™ got their name by combining the word *Questioning* and the word *Activities*. The idea for Questivities™ was developed when I (along with a group of my colleagues) noticed that project activities that had the potential to engage students in higher levels of thinking and rigorous learning were often done with little thought on the part of the student. Additionally, we noticed that students often spent more time making an attractive product than they did in thinking about what they were learning through doing the activity.

With the introduction of the Common Core State Standards, there is even more reason to emphasize higher levels of thinking when students complete short as well as more sustained research projects to demonstrate their understanding of the topics they are studying.

The Questivities™ format consists of a standards-based Project Activity along with a series of Thinking Questions that stimulate creative and critical thinking and give practice in research skills. The questions are starter questions that should be done before students begin the project itself.

Students who use Questivities™ before doing the Project Activity create projects that reflect higher levels of thinking, more creativity and more evidence of research. Questivities™ take students beyond just working on a project to thinking about the project ideas in more depth and greater detail.

Questivities™ can be used in many ways. They can be done individually, in partners or in a group setting. They can be a requirement used in conjunction with a project in a differentiated unit of study. They can be used to enhance and extend individual work and research. They can be one of several extension activities in a learning center. Questivities™ also make excellent alternate activities for students who compact out of the regular curriculum.

Questivities™ are assessed using mini-rubrics or other performance assessment criteria. Teachers can write Questivities™ for a unit of study or teach their students how to write and develop them for their own research projects.

Questivities™ are written on a user-friendly one page form. The form has the following elements:

- Project Activity which provides the focus for the Questivities™
- Common Core Standards
- Assessment Mini-Rubric for the Project Activity
- Project Questions (Essential Questions answered through the Project Activity)
- Questivities™ Thinking Questions
- Active Question

The **Questivities™ Thinking Questions** generally follow the following format:

1. List . . .
2. Compare and contrast . . .
3. What would happen if . . .
4. Would you rather.... And why . . .
5. How would you feel if . . .
6. Why . . .
7. How . . .

The 'List' question is a vehicle for brainstorming and opening the students' minds to multiple possibilities. On the other hand, the 'How' question focuses the student on how he or she will actually do the Project Activity.

The **Active Question** requires that students generate questions instead of answers. Some find this very challenging, especially students who always look for the one correct answer and think no further!

The Active question is a personification question in this form:

Make a list of questions ______________ might ask ____________.

The blanks can be objects, persons, places, animals, or anything else that connects in some way to the topic. It is amazing the amount of knowledge and understanding that is required to generate a list of such questions!

You will find the following Questivities™ in this section of the book:



At the end of this section is a blank Questivities™ form to use when you write your own Questivities™.

## Questivities™ - Constellations

**Anchor Standard: LA/Writing: Text Types and Purpose**
**Anchor Standard: LA/Writing: Production and Distribution of Writing**
**Anchor Standard: LA/Writing: Research to Build and Present Knowledge**

**Common Core Standards:**

- Write narratives to develop real or imagined experiences or events using effective technique, well-chosen details, and well-structured event sequences.
- Produce clear and coherent writing in which the development, organization and style are appropriate to task, purpose and audience.
- Draw evidence from literary or informational texts to support analysis, reflection and research.

**Project Activity**

**Create an original constellation using an existing star pattern in either the northern or southern hemisphere. Make a drawing of your constellation. Create a legend that goes along with your constellation that explains the meaning.**

**Assessment Mini-Rubric**

1. Constellation uses an existing star pattern
2. Drawing indicates shape of your original constellation
3. Story has clear and coherent writing with beginning, middle, and end
4. Story explains how the legend originated
5. Legend is connected to the constellation
6. Accurate writing conventions used

**Project Questions (Essential Questions answered through the Project Activity)**
What are constellations? Where did constellations come from?
How do legends develop about constellations?

**Questivities™ Thinking Questions:**

1. List the names of constellations that you can think of (at least 10)
2. Compare/contrast two constellations from those listed above.
3. What would have happened if myths or legends had never been told about the constellations in the sky?
4. Would you rather write a true scientific journal about the stars or write a legend about a constellation? Why?
5. How would you feel if we only had stars to use as navigational devices?
6. Why do stars twinkle?
7. How can you use your imagination to turn a star pattern into a constellation and a constellation into a good story?

**Active Question**:
Make a list of questions the **Big Dipper** might ask the **Little Dipper**.

Directions: Answer the Questivities™ Thinking Questions and the Active Question before doing the Project Activity.

## Questivities™ Designing a Structure Using Three-Dimensional Geometric Figures

**Math Domain: Geometry**
**Common Core Standards:**

- Draw geometric shapes with given conditions.
- Solve real world and mathematical problems involving area, volume and surface area of two- and three-dimensional objects composed of triangles, quadrilaterals, polygons, cubes and right prisms.
- Draw, construct and describe geometrical figures and describe the relationships between them.

**Project Activity**

**Design and draw a structure made from combining at least 4 three-dimensional geometric figures or shapes. Indicate area, volume and surface area of each shape. Label each geometric shape.**

**Assessment Mini-Rubric**

1. Design has at least four different three-dimensional shapes
2. Each shape is correctly labeled
3. Shapes are combined to form one structure
4. Shows area, volume and surface area of each shape
5. Design is original and could work in the real world

**Project Questions (Essential Questions answered through the Project Activity)**
What three-dimensional geometric shapes can be used to create an original structure?
How can we design and engineer structures to work in the real world?

**Questivities™ Thinking Questions**

1. List all the geometric figures you know (at least 10).
2. Compare/contrast two-dimensional and three-dimensional geometric shapes.
3. What would happen if the shape of the earth were a cube?
4. Would you rather be a triangle or a prism? Why?
5. How would you feel if all buildings were constructed in the form of pyramids? What would life be like?
6. Why are some structures in real life designed using one specific geometric shape? Discuss with an example.
7. How will you design your structure using four geometric shapes?

**Active Question**:
Make a list of questions a **Cone** might ask a **Pyramid**.

Directions: Answer the Questivities™ Thinking Questions and the Active Question before doing the Project Activity.

## Questivities™ - Graphing Calculators

**Project Activity**

**Write an article that could be published in a school or mathematics online newsletter about the impact of graphing calculators in the mathematics classroom.**

**Anchor Standard: LA/Reading: Integration of Knowledge and Ideas**
**Anchor Standard: LA/Writing: Text Types and Purpose**
**Anchor Standard: LA/Writing: Productions and Distribution of Writing**

**Common Core Standards:**

- Integrate and evaluate content presented in diverse media and formats, including visually and quantitatively, as well as in words.
- Write informative/explanatory texts to examine and convey complex ideas and information clearly and accurately through the effective selection, organization and analysis of content.
- Use technology, including the Internet, to produce and publish writing and to interact and collaborate with others.

**Assessment Mini-Rubric**

1. Clear and coherent writing
2. Correct spelling, grammar and punctuation
3. Explains the positive impact of graphing calculators and gives examples
4. Explains the negative impact of graphing calculators and gives examples
5. Accurate information and examples

**Project Questions (Essential Questions answered through the Project Activity)**
In what ways have graphing calculators enhanced understanding and/or extended learning in mathematics?
Are there negative elements to using graphing calculators in the mathematics classroom?

**Questivities™ Thinking Questions**

1. List the ways graphing calculators could be used in a school math class.
2. Compare/contrast a scientific calculator to a graphing calculator.
3. What would happen if students or society relied exclusively on calculators for all daily calculations? Would we develop as more advanced thinkers or underdeveloped thinkers?
4. Would you rather solve an algebra expression or graph an inequality using paper or using a graphing calculator? Why?
5. How would you feel if society had to function without any type of calculators? What do you think life would be like?
6. Why have various countries in Asia invested in their students having access to cutting-edge classroom technology at early ages?
7. How are you going to express your point of view in your written article?

**Active Question**:
Make a list of questions a **graphing calculator** might ask a **human**.

Directions: Answer the Questivities™ Thinking Questions and the Active Question before doing the Project Activity.

## Questivities™ - Immigrant Journal from the 1800s

**Anchor Standard: LA/Writing: Text Types and Purpose**
**Anchor Standard: LA/Writing: Research to Build and Present Knowledge**

**Common Core Standards:**

- Write narratives to develop real or imagined experiences or events using effective technique, well-chosen details, and well-structured event sequences
- Conduct short as well as more sustained research projects based on focused questions, demonstrating understanding of the subject under investigation.

**Assessment Mini-Rubric**

1. Written from the point of view of an immigrant
2. Historically accurate for mid 1800s
3. First entry explains reasons for immigrating to America
4. Three entries must deal with the journey to America
5. Six entries must deal with experience in America
    - Living conditions
    - Job availability
    - Attitudes of Americans toward immigrants

**Project Activity**

**Create a journal in the persona of an immigrant to America in the mid-1800s. Include 10 journal entries spanning a period of time just prior to your departure from your homeland and ending two months after your arrival in America. Decorate the cover of your journal in a way that reflects something about your homeland and your new home in America.**

**Project Questions (Essential Questions answered through the Project Activity)**

For what reasons did Europeans immigrate to America in the mid 1800s?
What hardships did immigrants face during their journey to America?
What hardships did immigrants face once they arrived in America?

**Questivities™ Thinking Questions**

1. List all of the reasons you can think of (at least five) that Europeans immigrated to America in the mid-1800s.
2. Compare/contrast the experiences of Irish immigrants and German immigrants.
3. What would happen if all of the descendants of immigrants were to suddenly disappear from America?
4. Would you rather be a Native American or an Irish immigrant in America in 1850? Why?
5. How would you feel if you were on your own in a large city where no one else spoke your language?
6. Why did some Americans resent the immigrants?
7. How will you design the cover of your journal? From what European country will you choose to be?

**Active Question**:

Make a list of questions (at least 5) that **an immigrant from the 1800s** might ask **an immigrant to America in the 21st century**.

Directions: Answer the Questivities™ Thinking Questions and the Active Question before doing the Project Activity.

## Questivities™ - The Water Cycle

**Project Activity**

**First sketch a design and then build a model that follows the same processes as those of Earth's water cycle. Using correct scientific terminology, identify and label each stage of the water cycle in the sketch of the model.**

**Anchor Standard: LA/Writing: Text Types and Purposes**
**Anchor Standard: LA/Writing: Research to Build and Present Knowledge**
**Common Core Standards:**
- Use precise language and domain-specific vocabulary to inform about or explain the topic.
- Conduct short as well as more sustained research projects based on focused questions, demonstrating understanding of the subject under investigation.

**Assessment Mini-Rubric**
1. Makes a sketch of the water cycle model with labels and captions explaining the processes reflected in the Earth's water cycle.
2. Uses correct scientific terminology
3. Water cycle is shown accurately
4. Follows Model criteria card

**Project Questions (Essential Questions answered through the Project Activity)**
How does water move through the water cycle?
How does the water cycle work?

**Questivities™ Thinking Questions**
1. List the processes involved in the water cycle.
2. Compare/contrast evaporation and condensation.
3. What would happen to the water cycle if the sun did not give off energy?
4. Would you rather be a cloud or precipitation? Why?
5. How would you feel if we ran out of water in your neighborhood or state?
6. Why is the water cycle an important process?
7. How can you make a sketch and a model that shows the water cycle?

**Active Question**:
Make a list of questions **water vapor** might ask the **sun**.

Directions: Answer the Questivities™ Thinking Questions and the Active Question before doing the Project Activity.

## Questivities™ - Wild Animal Habitats

**Project Activity**

**Draw and color or paint a wild animal in its habitat.**

**Anchor Standard: LA/Writing: Research to Build and Present Knowledge**
**Anchor Standard: Reading: Integration of Knowledge and Ideas**
**Common Core Standards:**

- Conduct short as well as more sustained research projects based on focused questions, demonstrating understanding of the subject under investigation.
- Integrate and evaluate content presented in diverse media and formats, including visually and quantitatively, as well as in words.

**Assessment Mini-Rubric**

1. Habitat is correct for the animal.
2. Animal is a wild animal.
3. Drawing has several details that show how the animal lives in its habitat.

**Project Questions (Essential Questions answered through the Project Activity)**
Why are habitats important to wild animals?
Why is the habitat of one type of animal different from the habitat of another?

**Questivities™ Thinking Questions**

1. List at least 10 wild animals.
2. Compare/contrast an eagle and a deer.
3. What would happen if the only habitat for wild animals was the ocean?
4. Would you rather see an animal in the wild or an animal in the zoo? Why?
5. How would you feel if you were the wild animal you will be drawing?
6. Why is an animal's habitat important?
7. How can you show details of your animal's habitat in your drawing or painting?

**Active Question**:
Make a list of questions **your pet** (or a friend's cat or dog) might ask the **wild animal** you will be drawing.

Directions: Answer the Questivities™ Thinking Questions and the Active Question before doing the Project Activity.

## Questivities™

______________________________

**Project Activity**

**Common Core Standards**

- 
- 
- 

**Assessment Mini-Rubric**

1.
2.
3.
4.

**Project Questions (Essential Questions answered through the Project Activity)**

**Questivities™ Thinking Questions**

1. List
2. Compare/contrast
3. What would happen if
4. Would you rather
5. How would you feel if
6. Why
7. How

**Active Question**:

Make a list of questions __________________ might ask __________________.

Directions: Answer the Questivities™ Thinking Questions and the Active Question before doing the Project Activity.

# TIC-TAC-TOE

## Tic-Tac-Toe Learning Activities

The Tic-Tac-Toe (sometimes referred to as 'Think-Tac-Toe') is a graphic organizer for standards-based student choice activities. Choices of learning activities are listed on a Tic-Tac-Toe grid or menu. This format is almost always a teacher favorite, perhaps because it is so familiar to all of us. Tic-Tac-Toe's can form the basis for a unit of work or can function as extensions of the required curriculum or as enrichment activities for a student's choice of a topic to study. This is one of the easiest ways to organize student choice activities and is very user-friendly. For these reasons, using a Tic-Tac-Toe is often how teachers start differentiating in their classrooms.

Students pay more attention and make better choices when the product or performance required for each Tic-Tac-Toe activity is underlined and boldface. This also helps you make sure you have been clear about what you expect the students to do.

The Tic-Tac-Toe format gives students some choice of learning activities, but also gives teachers some control in structuring the choices. If you give students a list of nine choices and ask them to choose three without using the Tic-Tac-Toe, many students will choose the three easiest, or the three requiring no writing. On the other hand, with the Tic-Tac-Toe format, you can direct how the choices are done to make sure that any set of choices will include a variety of types of activities. You can also ensure that no matter how the choices are set up, your students will be completing activities that address the Common Core Standards.

The Tic-Tac-Toe format is extremely versatile and can be used in any subject area with any age or grade level. While students usually complete products or performances using the Tic-Tac-Toe, the nine choices can be as simple as nine math word problems or nine vocabulary/spelling activities that can be chosen week after week to be done with different words. Examples of this in the Tic-Tac-Toe's appear in this book.

Because the configurations of activities can be so versatile, there are a number of different configurations in this book.

- Use the #5 choice as a Required Activity.
- Instruct students to complete one activity before doing others or after doing others.
- Have students complete one activity in each row.
- Base the student activities on learning styles or preferences.
- Choices can address many subjects or skills at the same time.

Like the student choice activities in the ILP™, it is important to keep track of the choices students make when using a Tic-Tac-Toe. Use a Tic-Tac-Toe Activity Chart with nine choices that can be checked off. On the next page is a Tic-Tac-Toe Activity Chart where all students were required to do #5 and then could do two other choices. On the following page is a blank chart to use with your own students.

# TIC-TAC-TOE STUDENT ACTIVITY CHART

| Students' Names | 1 | 2 | 3 | 4 | 5 | 6 | 7 | 8 | 9 |
|---|---|---|---|---|---|---|---|---|---|
| Abigail | ✓ | | | | ✓ | | | ✓ | |
| Aiden | | | ✓ | | ✓ | ✓ | | | |
| Alexander | | ✓ | | | ✓ | | ✓ | | |
| Anthony | | | | ✓ | ✓ | | | | ✓ |
| Ava | ✓ | | | | ✓ | | | ✓ | |
| Bob | | | | | ✓ | ✓ | ✓ | | |
| Chloe | | | ✓ | | ✓ | | | | ✓ |
| Daniel | | | | ✓ | ✓ | | ✓ | | |
| Emily | | ✓ | ✓ | | ✓ | | | | |
| Emma | ✓ | | | | ✓ | | | ✓ | |
| Ethan | | | | | ✓ | | | | |
| Isabella | | ✓ | | | ✓ | ✓ | | | |
| Jacob | | | | | ✓ | ✓ | | | ✓ |
| Jayden | | | ✓ | | ✓ | | | ✓ | |
| Madison | | | | ✓ | ✓ | | ✓ | | |
| Mia | | | | ✓ | ✓ | | | | ✓ |
| Michael | | ✓ | | | ✓ | | | ✓ | |
| Noah | | | ✓ | | ✓ | ✓ | | | |
| Olivia | | | | | ✓ | | | | |
| Sophia | ✓ | | | ✓ | ✓ | | | | |
| William | | ✓ | | | ✓ | | ✓ | | |

# Tic-Tac-Toe Student Activity Chart

| Students' Names | 1 | 2 | 3 | 4 | 5 | 6 | 7 | 8 | 9 |
|---|---|---|---|---|---|---|---|---|---|
| | | | | | | | | | |
| | | | | | | | | | |
| | | | | | | | | | |
| | | | | | | | | | |
| | | | | | | | | | |
| | | | | | | | | | |
| | | | | | | | | | |
| | | | | | | | | | |
| | | | | | | | | | |
| | | | | | | | | | |
| | | | | | | | | | |
| | | | | | | | | | |
| | | | | | | | | | |
| | | | | | | | | | |
| | | | | | | | | | |
| | | | | | | | | | |
| | | | | | | | | | |
| | | | | | | | | | |
| | | | | | | | | | |
| | | | | | | | | | |
| | | | | | | | | | |

## HISTORICAL AMERICAN HEROES: STUDENT CHOICE ACTIVITIES

**Anchor Standard: LA/Reading: Key Ideas and Details**
**Anchor Standard: LA/Writing: Range of Reading and Level of Text Complexity**
**Anchor Standard: LA/Speaking and Listening: Presentation of Knowledge and Ideas**

**Common Core Standards:**

- Analyze how and why individuals, events and ideas develop and interact over the course of a text.
- Read and comprehend complex literary and informational texts independently and proficiently.
- Make strategic use of digital media and visual displays of data to express information and enhance understanding of presentations.

| | | |
|---|---|---|
| **1.** Write an **acrostic poem** using the first and last name of one of the heroes you have studied. The poem should give information about this person and what he/she did to be a hero. | **2.** Make a **time line** representing events in the lives of 10 different American heroes who were champions of rights and freedoms throughout American history. Include dates from the 1700s to the present. | **3.** Design a **business card** for 5 of the heroes studied. Use 5 x 7 cards. List the rights and freedoms that they championed & the characteristics that helped them become successful in achieving their goals. On the other side make a **drawing** that shows one of the person's achievements. |
| **4.** Create a **collage** consisting of 3-5 word/phrases and 3-5 pictures/drawings representing one of the heroes we have studied. The phrases and pictures should symbolize their accomplishments and the time period and culture they lived in. | **5. Required Activity** **Read independently** a variety of Internet and print sources about at least 5 American heroes. **Take notes** as you read. Then **discuss** what you learned with a partner. Contribute your ideas to the class discussion about American heroes. | **6.** Create an **ABC Book** on one of the historical figures featuring his/her culture, time period, and the struggle for rights and freedoms that they supported. |
| **7.** Find a song from the time period that was used in the struggle for rights and freedoms championed by one of the heroes you have studied. Write a short **essay** about how the song captured the feelings, emotions, and determination of the struggle it represented. | **8.** Create a **life-size drawing** on bulletin board paper of an American Hero. On the drawing, list the 5 most important facts about his or her accomplishments. The drawing should represent clothing from the hero's time period. | **9.** Make a **poster** to honor one of the heroes studied. The poster should show basic facts about this hero, important events in his/her life, memorable quotes and accomplishments. |

**All students must complete #5 first. You may then choose any two other activities.**
**Name** ______________________________ **I chose:** ______ **&** ______

# TIC-TAC-TOE ASSESSMENT – HISTORICAL AMERICAN HEROES

| **1. Acrostic Poem**<br>Follows Poem criteria card___<br>Uses first and last name____<br>Correct format for Acrostic poem____<br>Gives information about heroic deeds of the person___<br><br>*Suggested extension: Find a poem by a published poet about a hero we have studied and read it to the class.*<br><br>**Possible Points ____** | **2. Time Line**<br>Follows Time Line criteria card ____<br>Has events from 10 heroes___<br>Dates range from 1700s - present____<br>Accurate information____<br><br>*Suggested extension: Heroes represent a mix of ethnic groups, ages and genders.*<br><br>**Possible Points____** | **3. Business Card & Drawing**<br>Has five hero cards____<br>Heroes' characteristics listed___<br>Freedoms & rights listed____<br>Drawing shows heroes' achievements____<br><br>*Suggested extension: Collect five business cards from local heroes of today and list the reason you selected each*<br><br>**Possible Points ____** |
|---|---|---|
| **4. Collage**<br>Follows Collage criteria card<br>Has 3-5 heroes____<br>Has 3-5 words/phrases connected to the hero ____<br>Pictures / drawings are symbolic of the heroes____<br><br>*Suggested extension: Include two biographical facts from each hero's life.*____<br><br>**Possible Points____** | **5. Required Reading, Research & Discussion**<br>Has at least 3 sources and notes from each____<br>Includes 5 heroes____<br>Participates in discussions with partner and whole class___<br><br>*Suggested extension: Analyze different points of view about one of your heroes.*<br>**Possible Points ____** | 6. **ABC Book**<br>Follows ABC Book criteria card____<br>Rights and freedoms the hero supported clearly shown____<br>Culture and time period of the hero are shown____<br><br>*Suggested extension: In your book, compare this hero to other heroes*____<br><br>**Possible Points ____** |
| **7. Essay about a Song**<br>Song is from the time period of one or more heroes____<br>Song captures the emotions & feelings from this period____<br>Essay well written with correct conventions____<br>Explains the struggle and freedoms gained____<br><br>*Suggested extension: Find a recording of the song and play it for the class*<br><br>**Possible Points ____** | **8. Drawing**<br>Drawing is life-sized____<br>Clothing drawn on the hero is from the correct time period____<br>Five important facts about the hero are listed____<br><br>*Suggested extension: Present your drawing to the class and explain the accomplishments that make this person a hero.*<br><br>**Possible Points ____** | **9. Poster**<br>Follows Poster criteria card__<br>Includes accomplishments, basic facts, important events & quotes from the hero____<br><br>*Suggested extension: Cite quotes about your hero from at least 5 other people. Include these in your poster.*<br><br>**Possible Points _____** |

**Name** ________________________________________________

**Comments/Feedback/Grade:**

## Ancient Rome: Tic-Tac-Toe Student Choice Activities

**Anchor Standard: LA/Writing: Research to Build and Present Knowledge**

**Common Core Standards:**

- Conduct short and sustained research projects based on focused questions demonstrating understanding of the subject under investigation.
- Make strategic use of digital media and visual displays to enhance understanding of presentations.

| | | |
|---|---|---|
| **1.** Create a **mosaic** made from small pieces of paper showing a scene during the time of the Roman Empire. Include a **written explanation** of the scene and its history. | **2.** Create a **collage** of the Punic Wars. **Orally explain** the items in your collage and how they give information about the Punic Wars. | **3.** Create a **time line** for Ancient Rome (509 B.C. – 476 A.D.) Include at least 10 entries that you feel are the most important events in understanding Ancient Rome. You can draw your time line or develop it on the computer. |
| **4.** Create a **scrapbook** showing at least 10 buildings or structures in Ancient Rome. Label each and show how they once looked and how they look now. | **5.** Make a **model** of an aqueduct (a structure used to transport water) in Ancient Rome. Explain in written form or orally how the aqueduct worked. | **6.** Create a **poster** advertising a "coming event" at the Roman Coliseum. Be historically accurate. |
| **7.** Make a **drawing** of both sides of a Roman coin. Include a written explanation of what is on the coin and its importance. | **8.** Create a **3 dimensional map** of Rome. Label the 7 hills. Complete your map by placing and identifying the Tiber River in its correct spot. | **9.** Create a **flow chart** showing the government of ancient Rome. Include at least six different positions (such as consuls, senators, tribunes, emperors, judges, tax collectors, mayors, generals, etc.) |

**I/we chose activities # ____, #____, and #____.**
**Name** ________________________________________

## Tic-Tac-Toe Assessment – Ancient Rome

| 1. Mosaic | 2. Collage & Oral Explanation | 3. Time Line |
|---|---|---|
| Shows a historically accurate scene during the time of the Roman Empire___<br>Has a written explanation of the scene and its history___<br>Follows Mosaic criteria card___<br>*Extension: Compare and contrast this scene to one in modern times.*<br>**Possible Points___** | Has several pictures depicting events during the Punic Wars ___<br>Has appropriate labels of events with dates and other information___<br>Oral explanation reflects research and shows knowledge of topic ___<br>Follows Collage criteria card___<br>**Possible Points___** | Has 10 or more entries___<br>Shows important events with explanation of why each is important___<br>Events between 509 B.C./476 A.D. ___<br>Follows Time line criteria card___<br>*Extension: Illustrate time line and include a bibliography.*<br>**Possible Points___** |
| **4. Scrapbook**<br>Shows at least 10 buildings___<br>Pictures show the buildings in ancient times and what they look like today___<br>Buildings are labeled with basic information about each___<br>Follows Scrapbook criteria card___<br>*Extension: Pick one building and show how it looked in each century between ancient times and the present.*<br>**Possible Points___** | **5. Model**<br>Historically accurate___<br>Explanation tells the location and function of this aqueduct and how it was built___<br>Integrates information as it is presented orally and visually___<br>Follows Model criteria card___<br>*Extension: Explain the engineering involved in building aqueducts.*<br>**Possible Points___** | **6. Poster**<br>Event is one that actually happened in ancient Rome___<br>Includes informative written text that explains ideas and information clearly and accurately___<br>Visuals are correlated to the written information___<br>Follows Poster criteria card___<br>*Extension: Poster includes an invitation to a reenactment of the event.*<br>**Possible Points___** |
| **7. Drawing**<br>Is an historically accurate Roman coin___<br>Writing tells at least five things about what is on the coin and why it is important___<br>Follows Drawing criteria card___<br>*Extension: Use heavy tag board and make replicas of a number of Roman coins. Create a game using them.*<br>**Possible Points___** | **8. 3-Dimensional Map**<br>Map is three-dimensional and includes all 7 hills___<br>Hills are accurately labeled___<br>Tiber River is in correct location___<br>Follows Map criteria card___<br>*Extension: Include other areas in the Roman Empire outside of the city of Rome.*<br>**Possible Points___** | **9. Flowchart**<br>Accurately shows the structure of government in Ancient Rome___<br>Includes at least six positions___<br>Shows relationships between the areas of power and influence___<br>Follows Flowchart criteria card___<br>**Possible Points___** |

**Name** ______________________________ **Comments/Feedback:**

## Bill of Rights: Tic-Tac-Toe Student Choice Activities

**Anchor Standard: LA/Reading: Integration of Knowledge and Ideas**
**Anchor Standard: LA/Writing: Production of Distribution of Writing**
**Anchor Standard: LA/Writing: Research to Build and Present Knowledge**

**Common Core Standards:**

- Integrate and evaluate content presented in diverse media and formats, including visually and quantitatively, as well as in words.
- Produce clear and coherent writing in which the development, organization and style are appropriate to task, purpose and audience.
- Conduct short research projects that build knowledge about a topic.

| | | |
|---|---|---|
| **1.** Choose a position regarding the second amendment and write a **position paper** to support your opinion. Make sure you have a number of facts and examples to back up your stance on this amendment. | **2.** Using computer software, create a **game** regarding the Bill of Rights. There must be at least 20 questions along with instructions on how the game is played. | **3.** Create a political **cartoon** or **comic strip** illustrating how one of the amendments in the Bill of Rights works. |
| **4.** Create **your own Bill of Rights** within your home and with your family. Include steps that will be taken when your rights are violated. | **5. Required Activity**<br><br>Write an **informative essay** about the Bill of Rights and provide an example for each amendment demonstrating your understanding. | **6.** Write and perform a **skit** with the courtroom as the setting when a citizen's right was violated by law enforcement officers. At the end of your skit, the class will act as the jury and make a decision based on the Bill of Rights. |
| **7.** Write at least 15 **questions** related to the Bill of Rights that you would have asked Dr. Martin Luther King regarding his treatment during the Civil Rights Movement. Include specific incidents that would have shown where his rights might have been violated. | **8.** Choose one of the amendments and write a free verse or couplet **poem** to show the negative effects if that amendment did not exist. Poem will be presented to class and must be at least 1 minute long. | **9.** Create a **newsletter** with at least three articles about incidents in your school where you felt that students' rights were violated and what you believe needs to be done to change things. |

**I/we chose activities # ____, #____, and #5 (Required).**

**Name** ________________________________________

**Due dates** ______, ______, ______

# TIC-TAC-TOE ASSESSMENT – BILL OF RIGHTS

| | | |
|---|---|---|
| **1. Position Paper**<br>Position regarding the second amendment is clear___<br>Has several facts and examples to support opinion___<br>Clear and coherent writing with correct spelling, punctuation and grammar___<br>*Extension: Debate the second amendment with someone who has a different opinion.*<br>**Possible Points___** | **2. Game**<br>Follows Game criteria card___<br>Game created on the computer___<br>Has 20 or more questions___<br>Questions are about the Bill of Rights___<br>*Extension: Play your game with a classmate.*<br>**Possible Points___** | **3. Cartoon or Comic Strip**<br>Follows Cartoon or Comic Strip criteria card___<br>Shows how one of the amendments in the Bill of Rights works___<br>*Extension: Post your cartoon or comic strip online where others can comment on it.*<br>**Possible Points___** |
| **4. Family Bill of Rights**<br>Has a list of 10 Family Bill of Rights___<br>These rights are fair to all members of your family___<br>Includes consequences when rights are violated___<br>*Extension: Share with your family and try living with them for one week. Write your evaluation of how well they worked.*<br>**Possible Points___** | **5. Informative Essay - Required**<br>Clear and coherent writing with correct spelling, punctuation and grammar___<br>Has all 10 amendments___<br>Has an example of each___<br>Accurate___<br>*Extension: Send your essay to your congressman along with a letter asking for his/her opinion of what you wrote.*<br>**Possible Points___** | **6. Skit**<br>Follows Skit criteria card___<br>Skit performed with at least one other person___<br>The right that was violated is clear___<br>Courtroom is the setting___<br>Case is made for and against the accused citizen___<br>Your class is the jury___<br>**Possible Points___** |
| **7. Questions**<br>Has 15 questions related to the Bill of Rights and the Civil Rights Movement___<br>Includes specific incidents in the life of Dr. Martin Luther King___<br>*Extension: Write answers to each of your questions, answering as you think Dr. King would have answered them.*<br>**Possible Points___** | **8. Poem**<br>Follows Poem criteria card___<br>One amendment is the focus of the poem___<br>Includes negative effects if we didn't have the amendment___<br>Follows Oral Presentation criteria card___<br>Presentation is 1 minute long___<br>**Possible Points___** | **9. Newsletter Articles**<br>Has three or more articles___<br>Focuses on incidents in school where students' rights may have been violated___<br>Explains ideas for change___<br>Clear and coherent writing with correct spelling, punctuation and grammar___<br>**Possible Points___** |

**Name** ______________________________________________

**Comments/Feedback:**

## BIOMES: TIC-TAC-TOE STUDENT CHOICE ACTIVITIES

**Anchor Standard: LA/History, SS, Science and Technical Subjects: Text Types and Purpose**
**Anchor Standard: LA/Speaking and Listening: Presentation of Knowledge and Ideas**
**Anchor Standard: LA/Writing: Research to Build and Present Knowledge**

**Common Core Standards:**

- Write informative/explanatory texts to examine and convey complex ideas and information clearly and accurately through the effective selection, organization and analysis of content.
- Make strategic use of digital media and visual displays of data to express information and enhance understanding of presentations.
- Draw evidence from literary or informational texts to support analysis, reflection and research.

| | | |
|---|---|---|
| **1.** On an 81/2 X 11 sheet of paper, draw the shape of a state with a fresh-water biome. Inside the shape, **illustrate 5 animals and 5 plants** indigenous to a fresh-water biome. | **2.** Create an **Information Cube** illustrating and giving information about plants and animals in the following biomes:<br>forest desert<br>tundra freshwater<br>marine grassland | **3.** Write a **fairy tale** about something that happens in the forest biome. |
| **4.** Write a **song** about plants and animals that can be found in the marine biome. | **5.** Choose a biome. Create a **diorama** using materials found in nature to depict plant and animal life in this biome. | **6.** Write the letters for each of the 6 biomes vertically. Then, create a **new word from each letter** that describes that biome. |
| **7.** Create a **comic strip** depicting an adventure through one of the biomes. | **8.** Create a **word cloud** using at least 20 words about biomes. Make the most important words larger in your word cloud. Log onto www.wordle.net to complete this assignment. | **9.** Research the tundra biome. Create a **museum box** showing the following details about this biome:<br>1. Animals of the region<br>2. Plants of the region<br>3. Landforms<br>4. Climate<br>5. Industry<br>Use:<br>http://museumbox.e2bn.org |

**I/we chose activities # ____, #____, and #____.**
**Name ______________________________ Due dates ______, ______, ______**

## TIC-TAC-TOE ASSESSMENT – BIOMES

| **1. Illustration**<br>Follows Drawing criteria card___<br>Has the shape of a state with a freshwater biome___<br>Has illustrations of 5 plants and 5 animals indigenous to this biome___<br>Accurate information and drawings___<br>*Extension: Do a similar set of drawings using a state with a different biome.*<br>**Possible Points ___** | **2. Information Cube**<br>Follows Information Cube criteria card___<br>Each side of the cube is about one of the biomes: forest, desert, tundra, freshwater, marine and grassland___<br>Accurate information___<br>*Extension: Make an Information Cube game to play with your classmates.*<br>**Possible Points ___** | **3. Fairy Tale**<br>Has a creative plot appropriate for the setting in a forest___<br>Characters have interesting things that happen to them in the forest___<br>Forest is clearly described___<br>*Extension: Find at least three fairy tales that are set in the forest. Write down the similarities you find in all of them.*<br>**Possible Points ___** |
|---|---|---|
| **4. Song**<br>Follows Song criteria card___<br>Tells about at least 5 plants and 5 animals found in a marine biome___<br>Song refers to how they live in this biome___<br>*Extension: Listen to songs about life in the marine biome. Make a list of these songs, what you learn from them and whether they are fact or fantasy.*<br>**Possible Points ___** | **5. Diorama**<br>Follows Diorama criteria card___<br>Focuses on one biome___<br>Uses materials found in nature___<br>Accurate depiction of the plant and animal life___<br>*Extension: Write a short report about this biome to go along with and explain your diorama.*<br>**Possible Points ___** | **6. Acrostic Words**<br>Each of the six biomes written vertically___<br>New word created from each letter___<br>Each word describes the biome in some way___<br>Accurate descriptions and words___<br>*Extension: Use www.tagxedo.com to create a word cloud using these words.*<br>**Possible Points ___** |
| **7. Comic Strip**<br>Follows Comic Strip criteria card___<br>Depicts an adventure in a biome___<br>Shows details about the biome in pictures, descriptive words and actions___<br>*Extension: Have the comic book characters travel to more than one biome.*<br>**Possible Points ___** | **8. Word Cloud**<br>Uses www.wordle.net to create the word cloud___<br>Uses at least 20 words about biomes___<br>Some words are bigger than others to show their importance___<br>*Extension: Make six word clouds, one for each biome.*<br>**Possible Points ___** | **9. Museum Box**<br>Focuses on the tundra biome___<br>Shows the following: animals, plants, landforms, climate, industry___<br>Uses http://museumbox.e2bn.org to create the museum box___<br>Has maps, pictures and text___<br>**Possible Points ___** |

**Name** ________________________________ **Comments/Feedback:**

## Black History/ Important Person: Student Choice Activities

**Anchor Standard: LA/Reading: Integration of Knowledge and Ideas**
**Anchor Standard: LA/Writing: Production and Distribution of Writing**
**Anchor Standard: LA/Writing: Research to Build and Present Knowledge**

**Common Core Standards:**

- Integrate and evaluate content presented in diverse media and formats, including visually and quantitatively, as well as in words.
- Produce clear and coherent writing in which the development, organization and style are appropriate to task, purpose and audience.
- Conduct short research projects that build knowledge about a topic.

| | | |
|---|---|---|
| **1.** Create a **5 W's chart** (who, when, where, what, why) and write a **newspaper article** about your person that includes important, unusual, and interesting information about him/her and his/her accomplishments. | **2.** Write a **business letter** to a museum or civic organization in which your state the reasons for your admiration of your person's achievements. Request that they honor him/her in some way, Must be written in correct business letter format with at least 3 paragraphs. | **3.** Write a **comic strip** where your person is the principal character. He/she should discuss with other characters his/her accomplishments and future plans. Make sure the dialogue is realistic and historically accurate. |
| **4.** Write a **song** in which you tell about your person and his/her major accomplishments. The song should have at least 3 verses. | **5. Required Research**<br>Choose an important person in Black History. Use at least 3 sources to find information about him/her including:<br>• Early life<br>• Problems encountered<br>• Important events<br>• Accomplishments<br>Take **notes** and have a **bibliography** with your sources. | **6.** Write and present a **monologue** written from the point of view of your person. He/she should discuss an important event in his/her life. Be sure to have your monologue reflect the probable emotions of your person. |
| **7.** Prepare **written interview questions** and answers in order to produce a 3-5 minute **video presentation** in which you dress as the person and pretend to be him or her. Ask one classmate to interview you and another to video the interview. In this interview, relate his/her important life experiences and achievements. | 8. Design a **poster** that includes the name, a center picture or drawing of the person with at least nine (9) important informational segments, clouds, or squares that contain information about the person's life and accomplishments. | **9.** Create an **illustrated time line**. Include at least 10 important events from the life of your person with accurate dates and illustrations of each event. |

**I/we chose activities # _____, #____, and #5 (Required).**
**Name** ______________________________________ **Due dates** ______, ______, ______

# TIC-TAC-TOE ASSESSMENT – BLACK HISTORY - IMPORTANT PERSON

| | | |
|---|---|---|
| 1. **Newspaper Article**<br>5 W's Chart (Who? What? When? Where? Why?)___<br>At least 3 paragraphs___<br>Accurate & important information___<br>Interesting news title to hook the audience___<br>Correct capitalization, spelling, punctuation and grammar___<br>*Extension: Post article online or in a printed school newspaper.*<br>**Possible Points ___** | 2. **Business Letter**<br>Follows Business Letter criteria card___<br>At least 3 paragraphs___<br>Explains reasons for admiring your person___<br>Requests an honor for person___<br>Correct capitalization, punctuation, spelling and grammar___<br>*Extension: Follow through with your request.*<br>**Possible Points ___** | 3. **Comic Strip**<br>Follows Comic Strip criteria card___<br>Has at least 7 frames___<br>Your person is the principal character___<br>Shows/discusses important events from his/her life___<br>Realistic dialogue___<br>Historically accurate___<br>*Extension: Make an entire comic book about your person.*<br>**Possible Points ___** |
| 4. **Song**<br>At least 3 four- line stanzas___<br>Follows Song criteria card___<br>Tells about person's achievements___<br>Correct spelling, capitalization, and grammar___<br>*Extension: Perform song in class or via a recording or YouTube video.*<br>**Possible Points ___** | 5. **Required Research**<br>Focuses on one person important in Black history___<br>Has notes in each of the 4 required areas___<br>Accurate information___<br>Has at least 3 reliable sources___<br>Correct bibliography format___<br>*Extension: Uses at least one primary source*<br>**Possible Points ___** | 6. **Monologue**<br>Follows Monologue criteria card___<br>Speaks from the point of view of the person___<br>Use emotional words and tone in relating an important event in the life of the person___<br>Written and oral presentation___<br>*Extension: Perform your monologue in class*<br>**Possible Points ___** |
| 7. **Video News Interview**<br>Written copy of 10 interview questions and answers___<br>Dress as the character___<br>3-5 minutes in length___<br>Answer questions about important life experiences and achievements___<br>Show video in class___<br>*Extension: Submit your video news interview to the Technology teacher for broadcast during the morning announcements*<br>**Possible Points ___** | 8. **Informational Poster**<br>Follows Poster criteria card___<br>Colorful drawing or picture of the person placed in center of poster___<br>Has nine important informational segments about the person___<br>Correct spelling, capitalization, punctuation and grammar___<br>*Extension: Write a short biography about someone who influenced your person.*<br>**Possible Points ___** | 9. **Time Line**<br>Follows Timeline criteria card___<br>At least 10 important events and achievements from the life of the person___<br>Correct sequence of dates___<br>Accurate dates___<br>Each event illustrated___<br>*Extension: Show other events going on during the same time period that did not involve your person.*<br>**Possible Points ___** |

**Name** ______________________ **Comments/Feedback**:

## ENERGY: TIC-TAC-TOE STUDENT CHOICE ACTIVITIES

**Anchor Standard: LA/Reading: Integration of Knowledge and Ideas**
**Anchor Standard: LA/Writing: Research to Build and Present Knowledge**
**Anchor Standard: LA/Reading: Key Ideas and Details**

**Common Core Standards:**

- Integrate and evaluate content presented in diverse media and formats, including visually and quantitatively as well as in words.
- Draw evidence from literary or informational texts to support analysis, reflection and research.
- Cite specific textual evidence to support analysis of scientific and technical texts

| | | |
|---|---|---|
| 1. Research the mining accident in the Upper Big Branch mine in West Virginia and the Deepwater Horizon explosion and oil spill in the Gulf of Mexico. Both of these occurred in April 2010. Write a **research paper** comparing and contrasting the loss of life, damage and problems created by each. | 2. Write an **editorial** about current issues with energy efficiency in America. State your point of view, give at least three detailed examples to support your point of view and end with a persuasive statement. | 3. Use the Internet **to research and collect data** about how much energy Americans use to heat and cool their homes, drive their cars and run appliances. Research data covering a one year time period. Then create a bar graph showing each month and the use of energy in each category. |
| 4. Create a **poster** advertising and promoting the careful use and conservation of non-renewable resources when producing and using energy. | 5. Required Activity<br><br>Read the chapter(s) in your science book that covers types of energy. Make a **list** of key vocabulary words and **define** each. **Outline** the main ideas and details of this chapter. | 6. Design a **game** to teach younger children about energy. The game should include both renewable and non-renewable energy sources. |
| 7. Write and perform a **skit** that shows at least five ways we use energy in our everyday lives. Include what might happen if we did not have sources of energy ready to use each day. | 8. Create an **Information Cube**. On the top, define renewable energy. On the other 5 sides, define and give advantages and disadvantages of the following types of renewable energy:<br>• Biomass<br>• Geothermal<br>• Hydropower<br>• Solar<br>• Wind | 9. Research ways to conserve energy our homes. Then write a **blog** that gives practical suggestions for conserving energy and encourages people to do it. |

**I/we chose activities # ____, #____, and #____.**
**Name** __________________________________ **Due dates** _____, _____, _____

## TIC-TAC-TOE ASSESSMENT – ENERGY

<table>
<tr>
<td>1. Research Paper<br>Accurate information on both accidents___<br>Compares and contrasts loss of life, damage and resulting problems___<br>Correct capitalization, spelling, punctuation and grammar___<br>At least two pages long___<br>Extension: Include another major accident that occurred while obtaining fossil fuels.<br>Possible Points ___</td>
<td>2. Editorial<br>Clearly expresses point of view regarding energy efficiency in America___<br>At least 3 examples___<br>Explains reasons for your point of view___<br>Ends with persuasive statement___<br>Correct capitalization, punctuation, spelling and grammar___<br>Possible Points ___</td>
<td>3. Data and Bar Graph<br>Has data showing energy uses for heating and cooling, cars and appliances___<br>Data covers one year___<br>Bar graph shows each month and the energy use in each category___<br>Extension: Collect the same data and make a bar graph showing energy usage in another country.<br>Possible Points ___</td>
</tr>
<tr>
<td>4. Poster<br>Follows Poster criteria card___<br>Promotes careful use and conservation of energy___<br>Focuses on non-renewable sources of energy___<br>Correct spelling, capitalization, and grammar___<br>Extension: Make several copies of your poster and hang in your school or community.<br>Possible Points ___</td>
<td>5. List and Definitions (Required)<br>Has at least 20 words___<br>Accurate definitions___<br>Has an outline of the main ideas and concepts in the chapter___<br>Possible Points ___</td>
<td>6. Game<br>Follows Game criteria card___<br>Game has at least 5 different types of energy___<br>Game teaches important concepts about different types of energy___<br>Includes accurate information___<br>Extension: Play the game with younger students or students in your own class.<br>Possible Points ___</td>
</tr>
<tr>
<td>7. Skit<br>Follows Skit criteria card___<br>3-5 minutes in length___<br>Shows 5 ways we use energy in our everyday life___<br>Shows what life would be like without these energy sources being readily available___<br>Perform for class___<br>Extension: Video your skit and put it on YouTube or a school or class web.<br>Possible Points ___</td>
<td>8. Information Cube<br>Follows Information Cube criteria card___<br>Has definition of renewable energy on one side of cube___<br>Other five sides include information about:___<br>• Biomass<br>• Geothermal<br>• Hydropower<br>• Solar<br>• Wind<br>Possible Points ___</td>
<td>9. Blog<br>Follows Blog criteria card___<br>At least 10 ways to conserve energy at home___<br>Explains importance of conserving energy___<br>Post on Internet___<br>Extension: Ask for others to add more suggestions on your blog.<br>Possible Points ___</td>
</tr>
</table>

**Name** ______________________________

**Comments/Feedback:**

# Government Branches and Levels: Tic-Tac-Toe Student Choice Activities

**Anchor Standard: LA/Reading: Integration of Knowledge and Ideas**
**Anchor Standard: LA/Writing: Research to Build and Present Knowledge**

**Common Core Standards:**

- Integrate and evaluate content presented in diverse media and formats, including visually and quantitatively, as well as in words.
- Conduct short research projects that build knowledge about a topic.
- Draw evidence from literary or informational texts to support analysis, reflection and research.

| | | |
|---|---|---|
| **1.** Construct a **diagram** that shows the three branches of government. Include an explanation of what each branch of government does. Incorporate symbols or drawings to represent each branch. | **2.** Create a **PowerPoint Presentation** comparing and contrasting the levels of government – National, State and Local. Emphasize what each branch does at each level. | **3.** List 5 different powers held by the state government and 5 held by the federal government, such as controlling the military or running schools. Make a **2-column chart**, one for each level of government. List the powers of each along with details about what each does. |
| **4.** On the Internet, find pictures of the White House, the Supreme Court Building and the U. S. Capitol. Then find pictures of corresponding buildings at your state and local level. Create a **slide show** where you compare and contrast the architecture, size, facilities, services, locations, etc. of each. | **5.** Choose any U.S President. Research facts about him, his accomplishments, disappointments and the era in which he lived. Write a **journal** this President might have written telling about his time in office. Your journal must have at least **6 entries** with dates and historical details. Remember, you are writing from the point of view of the President. | **6.** Choose one branch of the Federal government. Find out about the building or buildings in Washington, D.C. where this branch's work is done. Design a **brochure** featuring these buildings and telling the reader what goes on in them. |
| **7.** Create a **mobile** showing the three branches of our national government. Your mobile should have the name of each branch, functions of each and important people currently serving in each branch. | **8.** Write and perform a **poem or rap** describing the difference between branches of government and levels of government. | **9.** Make a **dictionary** of 20 government terms such as President, Washington, D.C., Constitution, Congress, Supreme Court, Capitol, laws, and taxes. |

**I/we chose activities # ____, #____, and #____.**

**Name** ______________________________ **Due dates** ______, ______, ______

## TIC-TAC-TOE ASSESSMENT – GOVERNMENT: BRANCHES AND LEVELS

| | | |
|---|---|---|
| **1. Diagram**<br>Follows Diagram criteria card___<br>Clearly shows the three branches of government and what they do___<br>Has symbols for each branch___<br>*Extension: Visually show areas where the two branches overlap and how this works.*<br>**Possible Points ___** | **2. PowerPoint Presentation**<br>Follows PowerPoint criteria card___<br>Shows similarities and differences between the three levels of government___<br>Gives examples and explains what each branch does___<br>*Extension: Show differences between county and city governments.*<br>**Possible Points ___** | **3. Two-Column Chart**<br>Follows Chart criteria card___<br>Has 5 powers of federal government and 5 for state government___<br>Chart lists the powers and details about each___<br>*Extension: Have more than 5 powers for each on chart.*<br>**Possible Points ___** |
| **4. Slide Show**<br>Follows Slide Show criteria card___<br>Pictures show the White House, Capitol and Supreme Court building and corresponding buildings at the state and local level___<br>Using pictures, compares and contrasts architecture, size, facilities, services and locations___<br>Accurate and well-researched<br>**Possible Points ___** | **5. Journal**<br>Follows Journal criteria card___<br>Focuses on facts, accomplishments and disappointments of one President___<br>Has at least 6 entries___<br>Written from point of view of the President___<br>Has dates and historical details___<br>**Possible Points ___** | **6. Brochure**<br>Follows Brochure criteria card___<br>Focuses on one branch of government___<br>Shows buildings in Washington, D.C. where work is done___<br>Uses descriptive words and pictures telling about the buildings and the work done in them___<br>**Possible Points ___** |
| **7. Mobile**<br>Follows Mobile criteria card___<br>Includes three branches of the national government___<br>Has the name, functions and important people of each branch___<br>*Extension: Include smaller offices or bureaus that are not well-known and put them in the correct branch on your mobile.*<br>**Possible Points ___** | **8. Poem or Rap**<br>Follows Poem criteria card___<br>Includes three branches and three levels of government___<br>Describes differences in the three___<br>*Extension: Perform or recite for your class.*<br>**Possible Points ___** | **9. Dictionary**<br>Has 20 government terms___<br>Alphabetical order___<br>Accurate spelling and definitions___<br>*Extension: For each word, include part of speech, pronunciation guide, and use the word in a sentence.*<br>**Possible Points ___** |

**Name** ______________________________ **Comments/Feedback:**

# LITERARY ELEMENTS – THEME, CHARACTER & SETTING: TIC-TAC-TOE STUDENT CHOICE ACTIVITIES

**Anchor Standard: LA/Reading: Key Ideas and Details**

**Common Core Standards:**

- Determine central ideas or themes of a text and analyze their development; summarize the key supporting details and ideas.
- Analyze how and why individuals, events and ideas develop and interact over the course of a text.

| | | |
|---|---|---|
| **1.** Create a **podcast** that analyzes the central theme(s) of the book.<br><br>(Theme) | **2.** Write and perform a **one-act play** based on the story. Make sure your play clearly shows the theme of the book.<br><br>(Theme) | **3.** Create a **montage slideshow** of images, music and text from the book that clearly develops and displays the theme of the novel.<br><br>(Theme) |
| **4.** Write an **essay** explaining how and why a character in the story is similar to you or very different from you.<br><br>(Characters) | **5.** Create a **diagram or web** showing how all of the characters in the book are connected. Include captions with **explanations** for each.<br><br>(Characters) | **6.** Give an **oral report** comparing and contrasting two characters in this story to two main characters in another novel you have read.<br><br>(Characters) |
| **7.** Make a **scrapbook** that displays the settings of the story. Include at least 10 pictures along with a **description or explanation** of each.<br><br>(Setting) | **8.** Construct a **diorama** that shows the most important setting of the story. On a large **index card**, explain this setting and why it is important.<br><br>(Setting) | **9.** Design a **travel brochure** advertising one of the settings in your story. Give details about what the place is like along with maps and pictures showing this location.<br><br>(Setting) |

**Complete one activity in each row (one for Theme, one for Characters, and one for Setting).**
**Alternate choice to substitute for any one of the above:**

- Create a trivia game that reviews all major literary elements. Include details from the novel in your game.

**Name** ______________________________ **I chose:** _____, _____ & _____

## TIC-TAC-TOE ASSESSMENT – LITERARY ELEMENTS

| 1. Podcast | 2. One-Act Play | 3. Montage Slideshow |
|---|---|---|
| Follows Podcast criteria card____<br>Themes are clearly identified____<br>Analysis includes specific references and examples from the story____<br>*Extension: Compare and contrast with the theme of another novel. Include this in your podcast.*<br>**Possible Points ___** | Follows Skit criteria card____<br>Actions and words in the play clearly show theme of the book____<br>Play stays true to the novel's characters and plot____<br>*Extension: Have someone video your play and show it to another class or upload it onto a website.*<br>**Possible Points ___** | Follows Montage criteria card____<br>Has images and video that clearly show the theme of the book____<br>Uses text from the book in the montage____<br>*Extension: Upload to an approved website so that students in another school can see it.*<br>**Possible Points ___** |
| **4. Essay**<br>Clear and coherent writing____<br>Correct grammar, spelling and punctuation____<br>Explains a characters similarities to or differences from the student____<br>Uses examples from both the novel and the students own life____<br>**Possible Points ___** | **5. Diagram/Web & Explanation**<br>Follows Diagram criteria card____<br>Clearly shows how various characters are connected to one another____<br>Accurate explanation of each character____<br>*Extension: Connect a significant quote to each character. The quote should demonstrate what the character is like.*<br>**Possible Points ___** | **6. Oral Report**<br>Follows Oral Report criteria card____<br>Highlights similarities between the characters in this story and another story____<br>Highlights differences between the characters in this story and another story____<br>*Extension: Include which novel you think has the most appealing characters and why.*<br>**Possible Points ___** |
| **7. Scrapbook & Explanation**<br>Follows Scrapbook criteria card____<br>Has at least 10 pictures showing the setting____<br>Each picture is described and explained in the scrapbook____<br>*Extension: Show how the setting affected the book's characters.*<br>**Possible Points ___** | **8. Diorama & Index Card**<br>Follows Diorama criteria card____<br>Shows an important setting from the book____<br>Clear explanation of the importance of this particular setting____<br>*Extension: Have two settings within your diorama and compare them.*<br>**Possible Points ___** | **9. Travel Brochure**<br>Follows Brochure criteria card____<br>Advertises a location that is one of the settings in the story____<br>Has details about the place____<br>Has maps and pictures____<br>**Possible Points ___** |

**Name** ______________________________________ **Comments/Feedback:**

## Scientific Method: Tic-Tac-Toe Student Choice Activities

Directions: Complete one student choice activity and then do Activity #5.

**Anchor Standard: LA/Writing: Text Types and Purposes**
**Anchor Standard: LA/History, SS, Science and Technical Subjects: Integration of Knowledge and Ideas**
**Anchor Standard: Writing: Research to Build and Present Knowledge**

**Common Core Standards:**

- Write informative/explanatory texts to examine and convey complex ideas and information clearly and accurately through the effective selection, organization and analysis of content.
- Integrate and evaluate content presented in diverse formats and media, including visually and quantitatively as well as in words.
- Draw evidence from literary or informational texts to support analysis, reflection and research.

| | | |
|---|---|---|
| 1. Construct a **flow chart** or **diagram** that teaches the steps of the scientific method.<br><br>(logical) | 2. Ask a question about a scientific problem. Write a **list** of 5 possible hypotheses that could answer the question or solve this problem. Pick one hypothesis and write an **explanation** of how you might test it.<br>(written/verbal) | 3. Make an **information cube** describing the six steps in the scientific method. Give an example of each step.<br><br>(kinesthetic) |
| 4. Write a **rap/song** that helps the listeners remember the steps of the scientific method.<br><br>(musical) | 5. **Required Activity**<br>To be done after you have finished one of the other choices. Use the steps of the scientific method. Write a **question** and develop a **hypothesis**. Then design a **simple experiment** to test your hypothesis. Look at your results and write a **conclusion**. | 6. Write and perform a **skit** or **play** about the steps in the scientific method.<br><br>(kinesthetic) |
| 7. On the Internet, find examples of how other students have used the scientific method. On the computer, type a **summary** of at least three of these examples and your **evaluation** of how well each used the scientific method.<br><br>(technology) | 8. Develop a **game** about the scientific method – play it with a partner.<br><br>(group learner) | 9. **Interview** (either by email or in person) a university science instructor about some research he or she has done or has seen someone else do. Ask how they used the scientific method. Write a **summary** of what you learn.<br><br>(written/verbal) |

**I/we chose activity # ____. I then completed activity #5. Name ________________________**

# TIC-TAC-TOE ASSESSMENT – SCIENTIFIC METHOD

| 1. **Poster or Flowchart** | 2. **List & Explanation** | 3. **Information Cube** |
|---|---|---|
| Follows Diagram or Flowchart criteria card____<br>Shows 7 steps of the scientific method____<br>Gives an explanation or example of each step____<br>*Suggested extension: Diagram shows other steps to do when hypothesis is incorrect.*<br><br>**Possible Points ___** | Has a scientific problem____<br>Has 5 hypotheses____<br>Clear and logical explanation of how the test could be done____<br>*Suggested extension: Choose two of your hypotheses to test for Required Activity #5.*<br><br>**Possible Points___** | Follows Information Cube criteria card____<br>Each side describes one step of the scientific method____<br>Each side has an example of the step indicated____<br>*Suggested extension: Make an extension to your cube to include all 7 steps.*<br><br>**Possible Points ___** |
| 4. **Rap/Song**<br>Follows Song criteria card____<br>Includes all 7 steps of the scientific method____<br>Accurate information____<br>Sing to class or on video____<br><br>**Possible Points___** | 5. **Required Activity**<br>Correctly uses all 7 steps of the scientific method____<br>Written documentation of each step____<br>Logical conclusion____<br>*Suggested extension: Has pictures or video showing steps.*<br><br>**Possible Points ___** | 6. **Skit/Play**<br>Follows Skit criteria card____<br>Includes all 7 steps of the scientific method____<br>Perform for class____<br><br>**Possible Points ___** |
| 7. **Summary & Evaluation**<br>Has 3 examples of how the scientific method is used____<br>Summary explains each example____<br>Evaluation gives logical reasons for opinions____<br>Sources of information from the Internet cited correctly____<br><br>**Possible Points ___** | 8. **Game**<br>Follows Game criteria card____<br>Includes all 7 steps of the scientific method____<br>Played with a partner____<br>*Suggested extension: Include other scientific information in your game.*<br><br>**Possible Points ___** | 9. **Interview & Summary**<br>Follows Interview criteria card____<br>Asks questions about using the scientific method when doing research____<br>Summary has clear and coherent writing with correct grammar, spelling and punctuation ____<br><br>**Possible Points ____** |

**Name** ______________________________________________

**Total points** _____ **Grade** ______
**Comments:**

## Sequencing Skills: Tic-Tac-Toe Student Choice Activities

**Anchor Standard: LA/Reading: Key Ideas and Details**
**Anchor Standard: LA/Speaking and Listening: Presentation of Knowledge and Ideas**
**Math Domain: Operations and Algebraic Thinking**

**Common Core Standards:**

- Analyze how and why individuals, events and ideas develop and interact over the course of a text.
- Make strategic use of digital media and visual displays to enhance understanding of presentations.
- Solve problems involving the four operations and identify and explain patterns in arithmetic.

| | | |
|---|---|---|
| **1.** Fill in a **concept map** showing ways you might solve a math problem or reach a goal. Then number the steps in sequence.<br><br>(Visual – Math) | **2.** Make a set of **flash cards** that need to be placed in the correct order to be understood. They should have a picture or word on the front and a written explanation on the back. This can be sequencing events in history, in a story you have read, steps in a science experiment, or a pattern in math. Number them in correct order.<br>(Kinesthetic-Visual-Verbal) | **3.** Create a **time line** that shows the sequence of events in a story, in history or in your life. Include at least 5 items.<br><br>(Visual – Reading – History) |
| **4.** Plan a **skit** to act out four parts of a story. Be sure to do the parts in order and indicate when one part ends and the next begins.<br><br>(Kinesthetic – Reading – Speaking) | **5.** Choose a topic you know about (such as how to play a sport, how to program a computer or Smart Phone, how to ride a bike, etc.) Make a **poster** explaining what you know using at least five sequential steps. Number them on your poster and use the poster to explain the steps to your class.<br><br>(Visual – Speaking) | **6.** Make a short **oral report** explaining how to solve a math word problem. Include visuals and at least four steps.<br><br>(Verbal –Visual - Math) |
| **7.** Write a 10 page **picture book** showing the steps used to solve math word problems. Include addition, subtraction, multiplication and division. Read your book to a classmate.<br><br>(Visual – Verbal – Math) | **8.** Create a **storyboard** showing at least six events in a story in correct order.<br><br>(Visual – Reading) | **9.** Use a computer to create a **flow chart** that shows the steps of the scientific method. You should have at least six steps in the correct order. Include a brief description of each step.<br><br>(Technological – Visual – Science) |

**I/we chose activities # ____, #____, and #____. Name** ____________________________

## TIC-TAC-TOE ASSESSMENT – SEQUENCING SKILLS

| | | |
|---|---|---|
| **1. Concept Map**<br>Has a main idea in the center____<br>Focuses on steps to solve a math problem or reach a goal____<br>Has at least 5 steps numbered in correct sequence____<br>*Extension: Do your concept map using www.spicynodes.org. Use this to present your ideas to the class.*<br>**Possible Points ___** | **2. Flash Cards**<br>Has at least 5 flash cards____<br>Each flash card has a picture or words on one side____<br>Each flash card has a written explanation on the back____<br>Cards should be numbered in the correct sequence or order____<br>**Possible Points ___** | **3. Time Line**<br>Follows Timeline criteria card____<br>Shows sequence of events in a story, in history or your life____<br>At least five events____<br>*Extension: Create a timeline using* www.readwritethink.org/files/resources/interactive/timeline<br>**Possible Points ___** |
| **4. Skit**<br>Follows Skit criteria card____<br>Acts out four parts of a story____<br>Indicates beginning and ending of each part of story____<br>*Extension: Have someone video your skit and post it on YouTube or a school or class website.*<br>**Possible Points ___** | **5. Poster**<br>Follows Poster criteria card____<br>Clearly shows what you know____<br>Has five or more sequential steps____<br>Presents information to class using the poster as a visual aid____<br>*Extension: Create your poster using* http://edu.glogster.com *and send it to your parents, your teacher and others.*<br>**Possible Points ___** | **6. Oral Report**<br>Follows Oral Report criteria card____<br>Clearly explains how to solve a math word problem ____<br>Has at least four steps____<br>Includes visuals____<br>*Extension: Use* http://prezi.com *for your visual. Include a video clip of someone solving a math problem.*<br>**Possible Points ___** |
| **7. Picture Book**<br>Follows Picture Book criteria card____<br>Has at least 10 pictures showing ways to solve math word problems____<br>Includes addition, subtraction, multiplication and division____<br>Reads book to classmate____<br>**Possible Points ___** | **8. Storyboard**<br>Focuses on one story ____<br>Has a series of at least 6 illustrations____<br>Events are in correct order____<br>Has a written comment, explanation or dialogue under each picture in the storyboard____<br>**Possible Points ___** | **9. Flowchart**<br>Follows Flowchart criteria card____<br>Shows the 6 steps of the scientific method____<br>Steps are in correct order____<br>Has a brief description of each step____<br>**Possible Points ___** |

**Name** ______________________________ **Comments/Feedback:**

## VOCABULARY 1: TIC-TAC-TOE STUDENT CHOICE ACTIVITIES

**Anchor Standard: LA/Reading: Informational Text: Craft and Structure**

**Common Core Standard:**

- Determine the meaning of general academic and domain specific words in a text at the appropriate grade level.

| | | |
|---|---|---|
| 1. Create a **vocabulary treasure map**. Map out a treasure hunt for your class using all of your vocabulary words in the clues. | 2. Create **vocabulary picture cards** with the word on the front of each card and a picture illustrating the meaning on the back. | 3. Pick a job you would like to have. Write a **resume** that would help you get the job using all of your vocabulary words. |
| 4. Create a 10- page **flip book**. Be sure to include all of your vocabulary words in the book. | **5. Required Activity**<br><br>Write the **definition** of each vocabulary word. Write a **synonym** and an **antonym** for each word. Write each word in a **sentence**. | 6. Create a **comic strip** using all of your vocabulary words in the captions or dialogue. |
| 7. Make **clay sculptures** depicting the meaning of each vocabulary word. **Label** each sculpture with the word or words it depicts. | 8. Compose a **poem** using all of your vocabulary words. | 9. Create a weekly **vocabulary calendar** with activities to help you learn your words each day. All of your words should be included within the week's activities. |

**All students must complete #5 first. You may then choose any two other activities.**

**Name** ________________________________________ **I chose:** ______ & ______

## Tic-Tac-Toe Assessment – Vocabulary 1

| | | |
|---|---|---|
| **1. Vocabulary Treasure Map**<br><br>Has at least 10 clues________<br><br>Clues use all of your vocabulary words ________<br><br>Clues are in order ____<br><br>Map is neatly drawn and gives directions/location of each clue ____<br><br>*Extension: Have your classmates do the treasure hunt.*<br><br>**Possible Points ____** | **2. Vocabulary Picture Cards**<br><br>Has at least 10 cards with 10 vocabulary words ____<br><br>Pictures clearly show the meaning of the each word ____<br><br>*Extension: Have pictures that show more than one meaning for each vocabulary word.*<br><br>**Possible Points ____** | **3. Resume**<br><br>Job you want is clearly stated on the resume ____<br><br>Resume indicates your qualifications for the job ____<br><br>Uses all of your vocabulary words ____<br><br>*Extension: With a classmate, do a skit where you are on a job interview explaining your qualifications. Use all of your vocabulary words in the skit.*<br><br>**Possible Points ____** |
| **4. Flip Book**<br><br>Follows Flip Book criteria card ____<br><br>Has 10 pages ____<br><br>Includes all vocabulary words used correctly ____<br><br>*Extension: Illustrations show meanings of vocabulary words*<br><br>**Possible Points ____** | **5. Required Activity - Definitions**<br><br>Correct definition for each word ____<br><br>Has an accurate synonym for each word ____<br><br>Has an accurate antonym for each word ____<br><br>Each vocabulary word is used correctly in a sentence ____<br><br>**Possible Points ____** | **6. Comic Strip**<br><br>Follows Comic strip criteria card ____<br><br>All vocabulary words are used in captions or dialogue ____<br><br>Meanings of each word are clear by the way they are used ____<br><br>*Extension: Comic strip addresses a controversial issue in current events.*<br><br>**Possible Points ____** |
| **7. Clay Sculptures with Labels**<br><br>All vocabulary words are included ____<br><br>Sculptures show meaning of words ____<br><br>Each sculpture is labeled with one or more vocabulary words ____<br><br>*Extension: Video each sculpture and your explanation of each.*<br><br>**Possible Points ____** | **8. Poem**<br><br>Follows Poem criteria card ___<br><br>All vocabulary words are used in the poem ____<br><br>Clear meanings of the words are clear ____<br><br>*Extension: Put your poem to music and sing it to the class.*<br><br>**Possible Points ____** | **9. Vocabulary Calendar**<br><br>Covers a week of activities ____<br><br>Has at least one activity per day to help you learn your vocabulary words ____<br><br>All words included within the week ____<br><br>*Extension: Help a classmate construct his or her own vocabulary calendar, explaining how you have used yours.*<br><br>**Possible Points ____** |

**Name** ________________________________________

## Vocabulary 2: Tic-Tac-Toe Student Choice Activities

**Anchor Standard: LA/Reading: Informational Text: Craft and Structure**

**Common Core Standard:**
- Determine the meaning of general academic and domain specific words in a text at the appropriate grade level.

| | | |
|---|---|---|
| **1.** Make an **illustrated dictionary** of your vocabulary words. | **2.** Make a **mobile** that illustrates your vocabulary words. Include a definition with each word/picture. | **3.** Make a **crossword puzzle** using all of your vocabulary words. You may use additional words if you want. |
| **4.** Create at least four **picture postcards** that illustrate your vocabulary words. Then use your words in the postcard message. | **5.** Create a **PowerPoint presentation** defining and illustrating your vocabulary words. | **6.** Make a **collage** showing your vocabulary words. Within the collage, label and give the definition of each. |
| **7.** Create **song lyrics and music** to tell about your vocabulary words. Think of a creative song title. Perform for your class and/or record and film your song for You Tube. | **8.** Pretend you are a reporter on the radio today. Do a three minute **radio report or podcast** using all of your vocabulary words in the report. | **9.** Create **Jeopardy questions** using your vocabulary words. Include 5 categories with 5 questions in each category. |

**Directions:**
**Do a different activity each week using your vocabulary words.**
- **Follow the assessment criteria carefully.**
- **If you finish the assignment, work on the Extension.**

**Name** ______________________________

# Tic-Tac-Toe Assessment – Vocabulary 2

<table>
<tr>
<td>1. Illustrated Dictionary<br>Has all vocabulary words spelled correctly____<br>Words are in alphabetical order____<br>Correct definitions for each word____<br>Illustrations match the definitions____<br>Extension: Dictionary shows parts of speech and an antonym for each word.<br>Possible Points ___</td>
<td>2. Mobile<br>Follows Mobile criteria card____<br>Has all vocabulary words spelled correctly____<br>Has a picture and accurate definition for each word____<br>Extension: Have pictures that show more than one meaning for each vocabulary word.<br>Possible Points ___</td>
<td>3. Crossword Puzzle<br>Follows Crossword Puzzle criteria card____<br>Uses all vocabulary words in the puzzle and spells them correctly____<br>Accurate definitions for each word____<br>Extension: Have some of your vocabulary words in the puzzle in more than one language.<br>Possible Points ___</td>
</tr>
<tr>
<td>4. Picture Postcards<br>Follows Picture Postcard criteria card____<br>Has 4 picture postcards____<br>Illustrations show meanings of vocabulary words____<br>Vocabulary words spelled correctly and used in postcard messages____<br>Possible Points ___</td>
<td>5. PowerPoint Presentation<br>Follows PowerPoint criteria card____<br>Correct definition for each word____<br>Picture goes with definition____<br>One slide for each word____<br>Extension: Uses animations to enhance meaning of words.<br>Possible Points ___</td>
<td>6. Collage<br>Follows Collage criteria card____<br>All vocabulary words, spelled correctly, are used in the collage____<br>Collage has labels containing words and correct definitions____<br>Extension: Place words in sentences within the collage.<br>Possible Points ___</td>
</tr>
<tr>
<td>7. Song Lyrics and Music<br>Follows Song criteria card____<br>All vocabulary words are included____<br>Creative song title____<br>Performed or recorded for class____<br>Extension: Teach your song to several classmates and have them sing it with you.<br>Possible Points ___</td>
<td>8. Radio Report or Podcast<br>Follows Radio Report criteria card____<br>All vocabulary words are used in the report____<br>Meanings of the words are clear based on what is said in the report____<br>Extension: Put your podcast on the Internet so others can download it.<br>Possible Points ___</td>
<td>9. Jeopardy Questions<br>Has 5 categories with 5 questions in each____<br>All vocabulary words used at least once in either the questions or the answers____<br>Accurate answers____<br>Extension: Play your game with a group of classmates.<br>Possible Points ___</td>
</tr>
</table>

**Name** ________________________________________

**Comments/Feedback:**

## K-2 Weekly Spelling: Tic-Tac-Toe Student Choice Activities

**Anchor Standard: LA/Language: Conventions of Standard English**

**Common Core Standard:**

- Demonstrate command of the conventions of standard English capitalization, punctuation and spelling when writing

| **1. Newspaper Letters**<br><br>Cut out **letters** from a news-paper or magazine to spell each word. **Glue** down on another sheet of paper.<br>Be neat. | **2. Story**<br><br>**Write a story** using 4 of your spelling words. Check for errors. | **3. ABC Order**<br><br>Write all of your spelling words in **alphabetical order** then each word **3 times**. |
|---|---|---|
| **4. Tongue Twister**<br><br>Choose five of your spelling words and write **tongue twister sentences** using each spelling word in a sentence. (Example: Pink pigs play the piano.)<br>Underline each spelling word. | **5. Sentences with Vowels**<br><br>**Write a sentence** with each word. Underline each spelling word and **circle the vowels**. | **6. Rainbow Writing**<br><br>**Write** your spelling words in pencil, making sure there is space between each letter. Then use three different **colored crayons** and trace over each letter so it looks like rainbow letters. |
| **7. Syllables**<br><br>**Write** each spelling word. Next to each word, write the number of **word parts**, or **syllables** it has. Example: together = 3 | **8. Code Writing**<br><br>Create an **original code** for each letter of the alphabet. **Write** your spelling words using this code. Example: 1=a, 2=b, 3=c, 4=d, 5=e. (bed=2,5,4) | **9. Pyramid Writing**<br><br>For each of your spelling words, **write** the first letter of the word, then on the next line, write the first two letters of the word. Continue doing this until you have the word spelled. **Circle** the vowels.<br>c<br>ca<br>cat |

**I/we chose activities # ____, #____, and #____.**
**Name** ____________________________________ **Due dates** ______, ______, ______

# TIC-TAC-TOE ASSESSMENT – K-2 WEEKLY SPELLING

| | | |
|---|---|---|
| **1. Newspaper Letters**<br>Has all spelling words____<br>Each word is spelled correctly____<br>Letters neatly cut and glued____<br>*Extension: At the bottom of the paper, write at least one sentence using three or more spelling words.*<br>**Possible points ____** | **2. Story**<br>Uses at least 4 spelling words____<br>Story has a beginning, middle and end____<br>Correct spelling, punctuation and capitalization____<br>*Extension: Use all of the weekly spelling words in the story*<br>**Possible points ____** | **3. ABC Order**<br>Words are in alphabetical order____<br>Words are spelled correctly____<br>Uses all spelling words____<br>Each word written 3 times____<br>*Extension: Create a dictionary using your spelling words*<br>**Possible points ____** |
| **4. Tongue Twister**<br>Uses 5 spelling words____<br>Has 5 sentences with most of the words in each sentence beginning with the same letter____<br>Spelling words are spelled correctly and underlined____<br>*Extension: Recite your sentences to the class.*<br>**Possible points ____** | **5. Sentences with Vowels**<br>Has a sentence for each spelling word____<br>Spelling words correctly spelled and underlined____<br>Vowels are circled____<br>*Extension: Also use spelling words from other weeks in your sentences*<br>**Possible points ____** | **6. Rainbow Writing**<br>All spelling words correctly spelled____<br>Each letter legible and neat with at least 3 colors____<br>*Extension: Create a picture or poster using your rainbow words.*<br>**Possible points ____** |
| **7. Syllables**<br>All spelling words spelled correctly____<br>Number of syllables for each word is correct____<br>*Extension: Teach your class a spelling and clapping game to show them the syllables in each spelling word.*<br>**Possible points ____** | **8. Code Writing**<br>All spelling words correctly spelled____<br>Has an original and creative code for all 26 letters____<br>Shows each spelling word written in the code____<br>*Extension: Write a short story using your code and give it to another student to figure out.*<br>**Possible points ____** | **9. Pyramid Writing**<br>Each spelling word correctly spelled in the pyramid format____<br>All vowels are circled____<br>*Extension: Make an artistic and colorful design from your pyramid spelling words.*<br>**Possible points ____** |

**Name** ______________________________ **Comments/Feedback:**

# TIC-TAC-TOE STUDENT CHOICE ACTIVITIES

**Common Core Standards:**

- 
- 
- 

| 1. | 2. | 3. |
|---|---|---|
| 4. | 5. | 6. |
| 7. | 8. | 9. |

**I/we chose activities # ____, #____, and #____.**

**Name** ________________________________________

## TIC-TAC-TOE ASSESSMENT - ______________________

| | | |
|---|---|---|
| 1. | 2 | 3. |
| 4. | 5. | 6. |
| 7. | 8. | 9. |

**Name** ______________________________

**Comments/Feedback:**

# Tiered Lessons and Units

## TIERED LESSONS AND UNITS

Tiered lessons or units are multiple versions of assignments and activities that permit students to work at their appropriate levels. Differentiation using this approach is based on differences in readiness, ability, skills, and/or experience. Tiered lessons allow students to build on prior knowledge and skills. The Common Core Standards and unit objectives being addressed are the same or similar for all students but are reached in different ways.

Tiered lessons are generally used with heterogeneous classes. They give teachers a way to differentiate curriculum so that the levels are appropriate for different types of students without being too easy and boring for some or too difficult for others. In a classroom with no differentiation, the needs of both higher- and lower- level students are not met. Struggling students worry about being a failure or looking 'dumb,' while high-ability students often become unmotivated and never develop the study skills or work habits they need. Tiering is a differentiation strategy that addresses both of these concerns.

A tiered *lesson* is usually taught in one or two days. A tiered *unit* usually takes a week or two. Thus, the amount of time working in a tiered format is up to you. Whether it is a tiered lesson or unit, the planning format remains the same:

- List of Common Core Standards and unit objectives
- Whole class activities
- Leveled activities (Levels 1, 2, and 3)
- Whole class culminating activities

The same planning steps are followed for a one- or two-day tiered lesson or unit of any length. Often the culminating activities will lead into new whole class activities and the cycle continues.

As much as is possible, make the leveled activities similar and parallel to one another. For example, when Level 1 students are doing a writing assignment, Levels 2 and 3 should be writing as well, just performing it in a more challenging way.

Higher-level work is not simply MORE work. It doesn't mean lower-level students write three sentences and higher-level students write 10 sentences. A key to developing higher-level work is to give students assignments with more depth (exploring an area of the topic in a more intense and profound way) and more complexity (exploring more aspects of the topic).

Remember the Coil Horizontal and Vertical Differentiation Model™ and the two arcs in the Introduction to this book. When using the Common Core Standards, all students should be challenged to use higher levels of thinking. This is true for Levels 1, 2 and 3.

## Levels for Tiering

For most tiered lessons, Level 1 is below grade level, Level 2 is at grade level and Level 3 is above grade level. Students are not necessarily in the same level for every classroom activity. Find the best level for each student to meet the learning objectives and standards of the lesson or unit.

Teachers usually assign each student a level based on their own best judgment or on the basis of some type of pre-assessment or skills inventory. These assessments can be formal in nature, such as a pre-test, or can be more informal such as an observation of students, a skills checklist, a brainstorming activity, or class discussion. You may also want to use KWL charts or webs that students complete to show what they know about a certain topic.

## Tiered Lessons and Units in this Book

In this section of the book you will find the following Tiered Lessons and Units:



At the end of this section you will find blank forms to use when you write your own tiered lessons and units.

## A Step-by-Step Approach for Writing Tiered Lessons/Units

Writing Tiered Lessons and Units so that the leveled activities parallel one another can be a challenging task. This step-by-step process works well. In the following pages is a sequential Initial Planning Form to help you as you plan.

1. Know the Topic for your Unit or Lesson. Write it on the form.

2. Establish which Common Core Standards and Unit or Lesson Objectives all students need to know at the end of this lesson or unit. Write them on the form.

3. Think about activities you have done with students in the past to reach these standards or objectives. Brainstorm with other teachers and use your resources to gather other ideas. Use the Initial Planning Form to make a list of activities. Write each activity on the first line for each item on the form.

4. Some of the activities on your list will most likely be easier than others. Label the level or tier you think each activity might be.

5. Decide which activities are appropriate learning activities for all students. These will become your whole class activities. Label these WC.

6. Think about ways to expand or extend the easier activities so they will be challenging for higher-ability students and ways to simplify the more difficult activities so that your struggling students can complete them successfully. Label these accordingly on the Initial Planning Form.

7. Make certain that activities at all levels are engaging and interesting. Nothing discourages achievement faster than students thinking that the other group is the one with the fun, interesting, or enjoyable activity while the learning activity they have been assigned is not.

8. Write your unit or lesson plan using the Tiered Lesson Plan format.

9. Check to see that the activities at one level are parallel to those done at another level. For example, are all students creating a visual, or are all students doing research? Tiered lessons are easiest to implement when activities at all levels are similar to one another.

10. Plan daily lessons based on your tiered lesson or unit plan.

11. As you would with any lesson or unit, gather supplies and resources needed to do the activities.

*On the next several pages are the steps to take when using the Initial Planning Form to create a Tiered Lesson.*

## Initial Planning Form for a Tiered Unit or Lesson

**Theme or Topic:**

**Common Core Standards:**

**Objectives:**

| **Possible Student Activities** | **Levels of Difficulty** |
| --- | --- |
| 1. ______________________ | ______________ |
| ______________________ | ______________ |
| ______________________ | ______________ |
| 2. ______________________ | ______________ |
| ______________________ | ______________ |
| ______________________ | ______________ |
| 3. ______________________ | ______________ |
| ______________________ | ______________ |
| ______________________ | ______________ |
| 4. ______________________ | ______________ |
| ______________________ | ______________ |
| ______________________ | ______________ |

# Initial Planning Form for a Tiered Unit or Lesson

*My Topic Here* ←

**Common Core Standards:**

**Objectives:**

**Possible Student Activities** | **Levels of Difficulty**

1. ______________________________ ______________
______________________________ ______________
______________________________ ______________

2. ______________________________ ______________
______________________________ ______________
______________________________ ______________

3. ______________________________ ______________
______________________________ ______________
______________________________ ______________

4. ______________________________ ______________
______________________________ ______________
______________________________ ______________

# Initial Planning Form for a Tiered Unit or Lesson

**My Topic Here**

*Common Core Standards Here*

*My Objectives Here*

**Possible Student Activities** | **Levels of Difficulty**

1. ______________________ | ____________
   ______________________ | ____________
   ______________________ | ____________

2. ______________________ | ____________
   ______________________ | ____________
   ______________________ | ____________

3. ______________________ | ____________
   ______________________ | ____________
   ______________________ | ____________

4. ______________________ | ____________
   ______________________ | ____________
   ______________________ | ____________

# Initial Planning Form for a Tiered Unit or Lesson

**My Topic Here**

**Common Core Standards Here**

**My Objectives Here**

*Possible Student Activities* ←  *Levels of Difficulty*

←

1. Standards based activity for topic ______ 2 ______

______ ______

______ ______

2. ______ ______

______ ______

______ ______

3. ______ ______

______ ______

______ ______

4. ______ ______

______ ______

______ ______

## Initial Planning Form for a Tiered Unit or Lesson

Theme or Topic:
*My Topic Here*
Common Core Standards:
*Common Core Standards Here*

Objectives:
*My Objectives Here*

| **Possible Student Activities** | **Levels of Difficulty** |
|---|---|
| 1. Standards based activity for topic | 2 |
| | |
| | |
| 2. *Standards based activity for topic* ⬅ | *WC* ⬅ |
| | |
| | |
| 3. | |
| | |
| | |
| 4. | |
| | |
| | |

## Initial Planning Form for a Tiered Unit or Lesson

**Theme or Topic:**

**Common Core Standards:**

**Objectives:**

| Possible Student Activities | Levels of Difficulty |
|---|---|
| 1. Standards based activity for topic | 2 |
| *Similar activity that is easier* ← | *1* ← |
| *Similar activity that is more difficult* ← | *3* ← |
| 2. Standards based activity for topic | WC |
| | |
| | |
| 3. | |
| | |
| | |
| 4. | |
| | |
| | |

## Initial Planning Form for a Tiered Unit or Lesson

**Theme or Topic:**

**Common Core Standards:**

**Objectives:**

| **Possible Student Activities** | **Levels of Difficulty** |
|---|---|
| 1. Standards based activity for topic | 2 |
| Similar activity that is easier | 1 |
| Similar activity that is more difficult | 3 |
| 2. Standards based activity for topic | WC |
| | |
| | |
| 3. Standards based activity for topic | 1 |
| Similar activity that is more difficult | 2 |
| Similar activity that is more challenging | 3 |
| 4. Standards based activity for topic | 2 |
| Similar activity that is more challenging | 3 |
| Similar activity that is less challenging | 1 |

# Tiered Lesson Plan: Articles of Confederation

**Anchor Standard: LA/Writing: Text Types and Purposes**

**Anchor Standard: LA/Writing: Research to Build and Present Knowledge**

| | |
|---|---|
| **Common Core Standards:** | 1. Write informative/explanatory texts to examine and convey complex ideas and information clearly and accurately through the effective selection, organization and analysis of content.<br><br>2. Gather relevant information from multiple print and digital sources, assess the credibility and accuracy of each source and integrate the information while avoiding plagiarism. |
| **Objectives:** | • Understand the limitations/weaknesses of the Articles of Confederation.<br>• Be able to explain reasons for calling a Constitutional Convention.<br>• Connect historical problems to current problems. |

| **Whole Class Activities** | **Assessment** |
|---|---|
| 1. Read basic textbook information about the formation of government under the Articles of Confederation. Take notes and answer written questions as assigned. | Has notes and questions as required.<br><br>Accurate and complete. |
| 2. Discuss the weaknesses in the Articles of Confederation. As a class, make a list of its weaknesses. | Class list has major weaknesses and problems.<br><br>All participate in discussion. |
| ***NOTES*** | |

| Level 1 Activities | Assessment |
|---|---|
| 1. Make a two-column chart listing the accomplishments of the Articles on one side and the failures on the other. Use the information from your textbook and from the class list.<br><br>2. Write a paragraph based on the information on your chart explaining whether you would like to keep the Articles or form a different type of government.<br><br>***NOTES*** | Follows Chart criteria card.<br><br>Has three or more accomplishments and three or more failures.<br><br>Paragraph is clearly written, accurate, and shows logical thinking. |
| **Level 2 Activities** | **Assessment** |
| 1. Gather information from digital and print sources to find out what reasons the founders had for calling a Constitutional Convention.<br><br>2. Create a brochure describing the problems of the Articles of Confederation and calling for a Constitutional Convention to solve those problems. Include reasons for the Convention that are historically accurate, clear, and persuasive.<br><br>***NOTES*** | Uses at least three sources.<br><br>Accurate information.<br><br>Follows Brochure criteria card.<br><br>At least three problems are detailed in the brochure.<br><br>Historically accurate.<br><br>Uses logic and persuasive language. |

| Level 3 Activities | Assessment |
|---|---|
| 1. Choose a point of view for a debate (see #2 below). Using print and digital sources, research arguments to support your point of view. Also, research the other side's point of view so you can rebut what they say. | Uses at least three sources.<br>Accurate information for your point of view. |
| 2. Participate in a debate on one side or the other of this topic: "We need to keep the Articles of Confederation and make them work" OR "We need to get rid of the Articles of Confederation and design a new government." | Follows Debate criteria card.<br>Reasons for your point of view are clearly stated.<br>Reasons are backed up by facts and examples.<br>Uses logic and persuasive language.<br>Historically accurate with evidence of research. |
| ***NOTES*** | |

| Whole Class Culminating Activities | Assessment |
|---|---|
| 1. After listening to the debate and sharing charts and brochures, the class will make connections with current discussions in the United States about the role and scope of government. | All students are engaged and participate in the discussion. |
| 2. Students will then discuss the structures of newly formed governments in the world today. Which problems are similar to ours at the time of our founding? Which problems are different? Is there anything we can learn from history that can help others countries today? | Connections are made between past and present, including the United States government and governments of newly formed nations. |
| 3. Students will then consider the question: "Is there anything we can learn from this period in history that can help us with our current political concerns?" As a class write a letter with thoughts and conclusions to your Congressman or Congresswoman and your two U.S. Senators. | Follows Business Letter criteria card.<br><br>States a point of view along with reasons for this point of view.<br><br>Has a conclusion and suggestions for congressional action. |
| ***NOTES*** |  |

# Tiered Lesson Plan: Integers

**Math Domain: Operations and Algebraic Thinking**

**Math Domain: The Number System**

| | |
|---|---|
| **Common Core Standards:** | 1. Use the four operations with whole numbers to solve problems.<br>2. Apply and extend previous understandings of numbers to the system of rational numbers. |
| **Objectives:** | • Using the Rules of Integers, students will add, subtract, multiply, and divide Integers.<br>• Students will use addition, subtraction, multiplication, and division of Integers to solve real-life problems. |

| Whole Class Activities | Assessment |
|---|---|
| 1. The teacher will show how to use number lines and absolute value to add, subtract, multiply, and divide Integers. | All students listen and participate in class discussion. |
| 2. The teacher will model and demonstrate addition, subtraction, multiplication, and division of Integers using the Rules of Integers. | All students have a copy of all examples in their notes. |
| 3. The teacher will demonstrate raising an Integer to a positive as well as a negative power. | |
| 4. The student will practice these processes by completing assigned worksheets and problems in the textbook. | All assigned textbook problems and worksheet problems are attempted. |
| ***NOTES*** | |

| Level 1 Activities | Assessment |
|---|---|
| 1. Each student will create an illustrated reference book showing the steps for adding, subtracting, multiplying, and dividing Integers.<br><br>2. Each book will show a real life problem that can be solved by each of the four operations.<br><br>3. Students will share their books with a small group during the Whole Class Culminating Activity.<br><br>***NOTES*** | Correct steps for adding, subtracting, multiplying, and dividing Integers are clearly shown.<br><br>Has a real-life problem for each operation.<br><br>Has a title, illustrations, and accurate information with no spelling errors. |
| **Level 2 Activities** | **Assessment** |
| 1. Working in pairs, students will develop a five-minute lesson teaching the Rules of Integers for addition/subtraction or multiplication/division to a group of students.<br><br>2. Visuals and practice examples showing how to solve real life problems must be included in the presentation.<br><br>3. Students will present their lessons to a small group during the Whole Class Culminating Activity.<br><br>***NOTES*** | Clearly explains the correct steps for adding/subtracting or multiplying/dividing Integers.<br><br>Five minutes long.<br><br>Visuals/sample real-life problems are included.<br><br>Follows Oral Report criteria card. |

| Level 3 Activities | Assessment |
|---|---|
| 1. Each student will write and illustrate two word problems for each of the four operations. These will incorporate real-life connections in each word problem and use both positive and negative Integers in each.<br>2. Solve each problem.<br>3. Students will present their word problems to a small group during the Whole Class Culminating Activity using number lines to help explain each word problem.<br>***NOTES*** | Has eight word problems, two for each operation.<br>All problems have a real-life connection and use both positive and negative Integers.<br>All calculations are accurate.<br>Uses number lines to help explain solutions. |

| Whole Class Culminating Activities | Assessment |
|---|---|
| 1. In heterogeneous groups with students from each level in each group, have students share and present what they have done.<br>2. After receiving feedback from the group, each student will evaluate his/her own product and make recommendations for improving it.<br>*3. Extension at any level: Make the improvements that were suggested during the small group feedback.*<br>***NOTES*** | Has written evidence of feedback.<br>Written evaluation includes at least two recommendations for improving their product.<br> |

# Tiered Lesson Plan: Money and Tax

**Math Domain: Number and Operations in Base Ten**

**Math Domain: Measurement and Data: Work with Time and Money**

| **Common Core Standards:** | 1. Use place value understanding and properties of operations to add and subtract.<br>2. Solve word problems involving money. |
|---|---|

| **Whole Class Activities** | **Assessment** |
|---|---|
| 1. Show pictures of items students might like to buy and determine reasonable prices for each item. Record on white board or chart paper using appropriate symbols and decimal notation. | Realistic prices written correctly using dollar sign and decimal. |
| 2. Discuss tax and how it is added to the total. Share a chart showing actual tax rates that are for their town. Demonstrate and have students practice adding the original price and the tax.<br>***NOTES*** | Participate in the discussion about money and tax. |

| **Level 1 Activities** | **Assessment** |
|---|---|
| 1. Choose 3 items, and add the prices together. Take the same three items, and add the tax for each. The teacher will give these students the correct tax for each item. | Correctly adds amounts using dollar sign and decimal. |
| 2. Solve word problems where the tax is subtracted from the total.<br>***NOTES*** | Accurate computation of prices without tax. |

| Level 2 Activities | Assessment |
| --- | --- |
| 1. Choose 5 items and add the prices together before tax. Assume two of the items are not taxed and the other three are. Add the tax to the taxable items. The teacher will give these students the correct tax for each item. Compute the total cost of all the items including the tax. | Correctly adds the items together using dollar sign and decimals. |
| 2. Solve word problems where the tax is subtracted from certain items in the problem but not subtracted from other items. | Accurate computation of all prices including those with tax and those without tax. |
| ***NOTES*** | |

| Level 3 Activities | Assessment |
| --- | --- |
| 1. Choose 7 items, three with tax and four without tax. Add a 10% tax on the three items, and find the total cost for all 7 items. | Correctly adds the items together using dollar sign and decimals. |
| 2. Solve word problems where some items are taxed and others are not. The tax is given as a percentage of the items' amount and students need to figure out what the tax actually is. | Students take the total and add the tax from the percent given. |
| ***NOTES*** | |

| Whole Class Culminating Activities | Assessment |
|---|---|
| 1. Students are in heterogeneous groups and are given prices of items to add together. This can be done as a game with different teams. | Correctly adds the items together using dollar sign and decimals. |
| 2. Give each group of students a certain amount of money and have them subtract to make change. This can be done on paper or with cardboard money. | Students need to subtract correctly using dollar sign and decimals. |
| 3. Whole group discussion: Why are some items taxed? Who decides how much the taxes are? What are the pros and cons of taxes? | All students participate in discussion. |
| ***NOTES*** |  |

# TIERED LESSON PLAN: RHYMING WORDS

**Anchor Standard: LA/Reading: Foundational Skill: Phonological Awareness**

| | |
|---|---|
| **Common Core Standards:** | 1. Recognize and produce rhyming words.<br>2. Demonstrate an understanding of spoken words, syllables and sounds. |
| **Objective:** | • Students will analyze and examine words understanding there is a recurrence of corresponding sounds at the end of words that rhyme. |

| Whole Class Activities | Assessment |
|---|---|
| 1. Demonstrate how two or more words rhyme by looking at a series of rhyming word cards emphasizing that the rhyming part is at the ending of a word and not the beginning. Write rhyming word pairs on chart paper. | All students look and listen to the teacher's demonstration. |
| 2. Listen to a story with rhyming words. Re-visit what makes two words rhyme. Re-read the story, and see if students can identify rhyming words just by listening. | Students listen quietly to the story and participate in helping to identify rhyming words in the story. |
| ***NOTES*** | |

| Level 1 Activities | Assessment |
|---|---|
| 1. Students match rhyming words using a set of rhyming word cards provided.<br><br>2. Using the rhyming word cards provided, students will write the 5 rhyming word pairs.<br><br>***NOTES*** | Cards are correctly paired with their rhyming counterpart.<br><br>Words are spelled correctly.<br>Word pairs rhyme.<br>All words are used. |

| Level 2 Activities | Assessment |
|---|---|
| 1. Using an assigned word family(s), create 5 rhyming word pairs.<br><br>2. Using a "cloze" sentence format, fill in rhyming words at the end of each sentence utilizing the word family(s) from Activity 1.<br><br>***NOTES*** | All word pairs rhyme.<br>Words are spelled correctly.<br>Has 5 pairs of rhyming words.<br><br>Sentences make sense.<br>Words are spelled correctly.<br>Completed all sentences. |

| Level 3 Activities | Assessment |
|---|---|
| 1. Identify and highlight rhyming words in an assigned poem. | All rhyming words are highlighted. |
| 2. Develop and construct a rhyming words story or poem using at least 5 rhyming word pairs. Sentences may not be the same sentences found in Activity 1. | Has original poem or story that used 5 rhyming word pairs. |
| ***NOTES*** | Rhyming and "word wall" words are spelled correctly. |

| Whole Class Culminating Activities | Assessment |
|---|---|
| 1. Share products from each level. | Group participation. |
| 2. Pass out rhyming word cards (one to each student) ranging from simple to more complex (i.e.: sat/fat, best/rest, bite/night). Students will walk around the room to find their rhyming match. Student pairs will share their rhyming words with the rest of the class. (Students who did level 3 activities will have more complex rhyming pairs, and students who did level 1 activities will have the simple rhyming pairs. | Group participation.<br>Found corresponding rhyming word. |
| ***NOTES*** |  |

# TIERED LESSON PLAN: STATE RESEARCH

**Anchor Standard: LA/Writing: Production and Distribution of Writing**

**Anchor Standard: LA/Speaking and Listening: Presentation of Knowledge and Ideas**

**Anchor Standard: LA/Writing: Research to Build and Present Knowledge**

| | |
|---|---|
| **Common Core Standards:** | 1. Produce clear and coherent writing in which the development, organization and style are appropriate to task, purpose and audience.<br>2. Make strategic use of digital media and visual displays of data to express information and enhance understanding of presentations.<br>3. Draw evidence from literary and informational texts to support analysis, reflection and research. |
| **Objective:** | • To learn about the geography, culture and people of a state. |

| **Whole Class Activities** | **Assessment** |
|---|---|
| 1. The teacher will introduce the unit by explaining that the United States consists of 50 states, each of which is different in some way. | All students listen. |
| 2. The class will create a KWL chart reflecting what they already know about various states. | Class participation. |
| 3. The teacher will encourage students to tell about their travels to other states and/or about their experiences living in other states. | Individual contributions with the rest of the class listening. |
| 4. Each student will choose a different state to research. The teacher will explain the method for choosing if two students want to study the same state. | Each student has a different state to research. |
| ***NOTES*** | |

| Level 1 Activities | Assessment |
|---|---|
| 1. Research your state using print materials and/or the Internet to complete the blank travel brochure (teacher-generated form) for your chosen state including its region, capital, state flower, bird/animal, important landforms, tourist attractions and other sites of interest, and famous citizens. | Travel brochure form is completed with the required information.<br>Includes pictures and a map.<br>Visually appealing and neat. |
| 2. Design a map of your state. Include the name of the state as a title, five cities (one being the capital), lakes and rivers of the state, and any mountain ranges or other landforms (examples: plateaus. plains, coasts, basins, etc.). Generate a compass rose and a map key drawn on your map to show what symbols are used for capitals, cities, and other items on your map. | Follows Map criteria card.<br>Has name of state on map.<br>Has all other required information.<br>Accurate. |
| 3. Create an acrostic poem using the letters in the name of your state (include one sentence per letter). Each sentence should tell one fact about your state – no repeating facts. Add color to your poem through either the state letters or a neatly drawn border or both. Be creative!<br><br>***NOTES*** | Neat with correct spelling.<br>One sentence per letter.<br>Accurate information about the state.<br>No repeated facts.<br>Colorful and visually appealing. |

| Level 2 Activities | Assessment |
|---|---|
| 1. Research your state using print materials and/or the Internet to create an accordion-folded four-page travel brochure for your chosen state. The brochure will be your own design. Include your state's region, capital, state flower, bird/animal, important landforms, tourist attractions and other sites of interest, and famous citizens. Your brochure should encourage people to visit your state. | Is accordion-folded into four pages.<br>Has all required information.<br>Includes pictures and a map.<br>Visually attractive.<br>Persuasive language. |
| 2. Design a map of your state. Include the name of the state as a title, seven cities (one being the capital), lakes and rivers of the state, any mountain ranges or other landforms (examples: plateaus, plains, coasts, basins, etc.), state parks, and unique historical sites. Generate a compass rose and a map key drawn on your map to show what symbols are used for capitals, cities, and other items on your map. | Follows Map criteria card.<br>Has name of state on map.<br>Has all other required information.<br>Accurate. |
| 3. Create an illustrated ABC book highlighting important facts about your state and places or things that visitors to your state would want to visit. Mention at least one city to visit and why. Give the book a title, and use captions to describe each of the pictures. Pictures can be hand-drawn or cut out of magazines, newspapers, or taken from the Internet. Your book can be handwritten or computer generated.<br><br>***NOTES*** | Follows ABC Book criteria card.<br>Tells about places of interest, important facts, and at least one city.<br>Visuals contribute to understanding the information. |

| **Level 3 Activities** | **Assessment** |
| --- | --- |
| 1. Research your state using print materials and/or the internet to design a six-page travel booklet (student-generated, including front and back covers) for your chosen state including when and how it became a state, major events in the state's history, its region, capital, state flower, bird/animal, important landforms, tourist attractions and other sites of interest, and famous citizens. Include at least two interesting facts about your state that most people do not know. | Has 6 pages including a front and back cover<br>Has all required information.<br>Includes pictures and other visuals.<br>Accurate information.<br>Visually attractive. |
| 2. Design a map of your state. Include the name of the state as a title, ten cities (one being the capital), lakes and rivers of the state, any mountain ranges or other landforms (examples: plateaus, plains, coasts, basins, etc.). Generate a compass rose, a map key, and map scale drawn on your map to show what symbols are used for capitals, cities, and other items on your map. Include miles per inch with your map scale. | Follows Map criteria card.<br>Has the name of the state on the map.<br>Has all required information.<br>Accurate information.<br>Map scale is accurate. |
| 3. Generate at least four ideas about why places in your state would be a great spots for a vacation. You will need to list your ideas clearly and then explain why your ideas would persuade someone to visit your state for a vacation. Using this list of ideas, write a persuasive essay telling people why they should visit your state. Your essay must be at least three paragraphs long and have an illustration or picture supporting each of your ideas. | Three paragraphs in essay.<br>Clear and coherent writing.<br>Correct grammar, spelling, and punctuation.<br>Has at least 4 ideas about why your state is a good vacation location.<br>Illustration for each idea. |
| ***NOTES*** | |

| Whole Class Culminating Activities | Assessment |
|---|---|
| 1. In heterogeneous groups, students will share their travel brochures and booklets. Each group member will show and explain his/her product to the group. | All group members listen to one another and share their work. |
| 2. Students will present their state maps to the class pointing out the required information. All of the students' state maps will be combined to create the entire map of the US that will be displayed on a classroom wall. | Maps will follow the stated criteria, and students will speak clearly when explaining their maps to the class.<br><br>Students in the audience will be respectful of the presenter. |
| 3. In heterogeneous groups, students will share their visual and written word products: acrostic poems, ABC books, and persuasive essays with illustrations. | All group members listen to one another and share their work. |
| ***NOTES*** |  |

# Tiered Lesson Plan: Jar of Synonyms

**Anchor Standard: Language Arts: Vocabulary Acquisition and Use**

| **Common Core Standard:** | Determine or clarify the meaning of unknown and multiple-meaning words and phrases by using context clues, analyzing meaningful word parts and consulting general and specialized reference materials as appropriate. |
|---|---|

| **Whole Class Activities** | **Assessment** |
|---|---|
| 1. The teacher will review the meaning of the word *synonym.* | All students are paying attention. |
| 2. The teacher will demonstrate with the class how to use a thesaurus to find synonyms for a word. | All students are observing teacher's demonstration. |
| 3. The teacher will discuss the fact that some words are overused in writing so we want to replace these words when possible. | |
| 4. The class will brainstorm a list of overused words. | All students help brainstorm list of overused words. |
| ***NOTES*** | |

| Level 1 Activities | Assessment |
| --- | --- |
| 1. Students will be given a colored poster board that is cut in the shape of a giant jar, 5 white circles to write on, and 5 sentence strips. | |
| 2. The students will work in a group. The group will choose 5 words from the list brainstormed in class and write each word on a white circle using a different color marker. | The students each have 5 words written from the class list.<br><br>The words are written in different colors. |
| 3. The students will each have a thesaurus and work as a group with the teacher to look up each word. When the word is found in the thesaurus, the students will write the synonyms on the circles using the same color marker that was used for the original word. | The students each have 4 synonyms for each word.<br><br>The synonyms are written in the same color as the original word. |
| 4. The students will then work independently to generate a sentence using one of the synonyms for each word in the circles. Each student will write these sentences on their sentence strips.<br><br>***NOTES*** | The students each have 5 sentences correctly copied.<br><br>Each sentence has a synonym from a different word.<br><br>Each sentence has a capital letter and a punctuation mark. |

| Level 2 Activities | Assessment |
|---|---|
| 1. The students will be given a colored poster board that is cut in the shape of a giant jar, they will be given white circles to write on, and 5 sentence strips. | |
| 2. The students will work with a partner. They will choose 3 words from the list brainstormed in class and 2 words that they choose together. They will write each word on a white circle using a different color marker. | The students each have 3 words written from the class list.<br><br>The students each have 2 choice words written.<br><br>The words are written in different colors. |
| 3. The students will each have a thesaurus and work together to look up each word. When the word is found in the thesaurus, the students will write 4 synonyms on the circles (one word per circle) using the same color marker that was used for the original word. | The students each have 4 synonyms for each word.<br><br>The synonyms are written n the same color as the original word. |
| 4. The students will then work together to come up with a sentence using a synonym for each set of words. They will write their sentences on their sentence strips.<br><br>***NOTES*** | The students each have 5 sentences written.<br><br>Each sentence has a synonym from a different group.<br><br>Each sentence has a capital letter and a punctuation mark. |

| Level 3 Activities | Assessment |
|---|---|
| 1. The students will be given a colored poster board that is cut in the shape of a giant jar, white circles to write on, and 5 sentence strips. | |
| 2. The students will work independently. The student will choose 2 words from the list brainstormed in class and 3 words on his/her own. The student will write each word on a white circle using a different color marker. | The student has 2 words written from the class list.<br><br>The student has 3 choice words written.<br><br>The words are written in different colors. |
| 3. The student will use a thesaurus to look up each word. When the word is found in the thesaurus, the student will write 4 synonyms on the circles (one word per circle) using the same color marker that was used for the original word and one antonym in a different color. | The student has 4 synonyms and one antonym for each word.<br><br>The synonyms are written in the same color as the original word. |
| 4. The student will then generate a sentence using one synonym and one antonym for each set of words. The student will write the sentences on his/her sentence strips.<br><br>***NOTES*** | The student has 5 sentences written.<br><br>Each sentence has a synonym and an antonym from a different group.<br><br>Each sentence has a capital letter and a punctuation mark. |

| **Whole Class Culminating Activities** | **Assessment** |
| --- | --- |
| 1. Students will work in heterogeneous groups reading the words in their jar of synonyms to each other and reading their sentences to each other.<br><br>2. Students will add at least 5 words that they have learned today to their personal writing dictionaries.<br><br>***NOTES*** | Group participation.<br><br>Ability to read own writing.<br><br>Ability to listen to others.<br><br>On task behavior.<br><br>Students have added 5 words to their personal writing dictionaries.<br><br> |

# Tiered Lesson Plan: Whole Number Division with Remainders

**Math Domain: Number and Operation in Base Ten**

| | |
|---|---|
| **Common Core Standard:** | Find whole-number quotients and remainders with up to four digit dividends and one digit divisors. Use strategies based on place value, the properties of operations and/or the relationship between multiplication and division. |
| **Objectives:** | • Students will successfully solve whole number division problems.<br>• Students will correctly express the remainders in division problems as fractions and the answers as mixed numbers. |

| Whole Class Activities | Assessment |
|---|---|
| 1. Model division problems using the partial-quotients method for division. Demonstrate rewriting the remainders as fractions and the answers as mixed numbers. | Students watch and listen to the teacher's demonstration. |
| 2. Write a few division problems on the board and include the answers to the problems written with remainders. Have students use paper, individual white boards, or any digital method to rewrite the remainders as fractions and their answers as mixed numbers. | Informal observation.<br><br>Students actively participate.<br><br>Correct answers recorded on paper, whiteboards, or digitally. |
| ***NOTES*** | |

| Level 1 Activities | Assessment |
|---|---|
| 1. Have these students work in a small group with you. Work together to solve whole number division problems and to report the answers as mixed numbers. | Students actively participate.<br><br>Students correctly follow the steps for the division method. |
| 2. Begin with two-digit numbers divided by one-digit numbers and proceed to three-digit numbers divided by one-digit numbers. You can use the "card method" to generate the division problems as described in the Level 2 activities. | Accurate quotients with remainders rewritten as fractions and answers written as mixed numbers. |
| 3. Assess frequently. As two students are ready, move them as partners to Level 2 activities.<br><br>***NOTES*** | |

| Level 2 Activities | Assessment |
|---|---|
| 1. Students work with partners and use the "card method" (ten index cards each with one number from 0-9 on it) to generate division problems. | Worksheet from card method with accurate quotients and remainders rewritten as fractions and answers written as mixed numbers. |
| 2. Students turn over 3 cards in a row (dividend) and a $4^{th}$ card (divisor). Partners write the problems and answer before they proceed to the next problem. If they disagree, partners take turns explaining their work to each other and attempt to find the correct solution. Do 10 problems.<br><br>***NOTES*** | Work on scratch paper is consistent with and supports the reported answers. |

| Level 3 Activities | Assessment |
|---|---|
| 1. Students work with partners to create and solve at least 5 division number stories. Each story should require division of three- or four-digit dividends with a remainder. When the problems are created and solved, each pair will trade stories with another Level 3 pair and attempt to solve the problems they have been given.<br><br>2. Pairs will provide feedback to each other as to whether or not the number stories contain three- or four-digit division problems and whether each number story makes sense or needs to be clarified. Students will then have the opportunity to make revisions if necessary.<br><br>***NOTES*** | Number stories require three- and four-digit division with remainders.<br><br>Solutions are accurate – remainders are rewritten as fractions and answers are written as mixed numbers. |

| Whole Class Culminating Activities | Assessment |
|---|---|
| 1. Students complete a reflection on the lesson.<br>a. Tell me how you feel you are doing with division. What are you still confused about? Do you feel like you are doing better than when we first started? Be honest.<br>or<br>b. What did you think was the best part of today's activities on division? What was hardest for you?<br><br>2. Students volunteer to share their reflections.<br><br>***NOTES*** | Student responds to prompt (at least 2 sentences).<br><br>Students participate and listen to others.<br><br> |

## Tiered Lesson Plan: Writing a Picture Book Narrative (K-2)

**Anchor Standard: Writing: Text Types and Purposes**

| | |
|---|---|
| **Common Core Standard:** | Write narratives to develop real or imagined experiences or events using effective technique, well-chosen details, and well-structured event sequences. |
| **Objectives:** | • Students will be able to write a personal narrative about a small event in their lives on four pages of a picture book.<br>• Students will be able to read their stories in a small group setting. |

| Whole Class Activities | Assessment |
|---|---|
| 1. Read a picture book to the class that has lots of details in both the pictures and the words.<br><br>2. Discuss how the story is told through the pictures and words of the book and how important these details are.<br><br>3. Share a 'small moment' with the class. For example, *"Yesterday, when I was riding my bike, I saw two squirrels chasing each other up a tree!"* Use a 4-page paper booklet to touch each page and tell the story. Be sure to add details as you touch each page.<br><br>4. Now, go back to the first page, and ask the students what happened at the beginning of your story. Draw the picture as students dictate to you details from your oral story.<br><br>5. Continue on for pages 2 and 3.<br><br>6. Brainstorm words and sentences that could go along with the pictures to tell the story.<br><br>7. Distribute a blank 4-page booklet to each student. Ask students to think of a small moment from their lives. Have them share their stories with their partners while touching each page of their booklets. Partners do not have to be on the same level. | Students answer questions and give examples during group discussion.<br><br>Students plan their personal narratives by thinking of and identifying a 'small moment' from their own lives.<br><br>Students share their stories with their partners by touching each page of their booklets and saying what happens on each page. |

| Level 1 Activities | Assessment |
|---|---|
| 1. Use the first page as a title page with the title, your name and an illustration for your story.<br><br>2. Write your small moment across the other three pages of your booklet. The writing is in the form of pictures and a few words. Add details so that we can see and you can read to us the story when you finish! Label your pictures. (example – the letter "D" or the word "Dog" next to the picture of a dog)<br><br>***NOTES*** | There is a title page with the title of the story, a picture, and the author's name.<br><br>The student uses pictures and a few words (at least one word per page) to tell a cohesive story with a clear beginning, middle, and ending. |
| **Level 2 Activities** | **Assessment** |
| 1. Use the first page as a title page with the title, your name and an illustration for your story.<br><br>2. Write your small moment across the other three pages of your booklet. Each page should have at least one picture and one sentence at the bottom of the page that tells what is happening in the picture.<br><br>***NOTES*** | There is a title page with the title of the story, a picture, and the author's name.<br><br>Students write a cohesive story with a beginning, middle, and ending. Books include a picture and a single sentence at the bottom of each page telling what is happening. Sentences should have details that explain each picture. |

| Level 3 Activities | Assessment |
|---|---|
| 1. Use the first page as a title page with the title, your name and an illustration for your story. | There is a title page with the title of the story, a picture, and the author's name. |
| 2. Write your small moment across the three page booklet with a picture and two or more detailed sentences at the bottom of each page. Use descriptive words in your story and make sure your sentences match what is happening in the picture. Be sure to have a closure at the end of your story.<br><br>***NOTES*** | Students write a cohesive story with a beginning, middle, and ending. Students sketch their pictures and write complete sentences at the bottom of each page telling the story. Students write 2+ sentences per page adding needed details. |
| **Whole Class Culminating Activities** | **Assessment** |
| 1. In groups of three, students will share their stories. Each student will show and read their story to the other members of their group.<br><br>***NOTES*** | Students will listen to one another and share their work.<br><br> |

# TIERED LESSON PLAN: UNIT PLANNING FORM

**COMMON CORE STANDARDS**

**OBJECTIVES**

1.
2.
3.
4.

**Whole Class Activities**

**Assessment**

**Level 1 Activities**

**Assessment**

**Level 2 Activities**

**Assessment**

**Level 3 Activities**

**Assessment**

**Whole Class Culminating Activities**

**Assessment**

# Index of Products

# Index of Common Core Standards

The Common Core State Standards used in *Differentiated Activities and Assessments Using the Common Core Standards* are listed below in first-word alphabetical order for ease in finding activities and products within the Criteria Cards, Curriculum Compactors, ILP™s, Questivities™, Tic-Tac-Toes, and Tiered Lessons.

## Anchor Standards, Math Domains, and Literacy in History, Social Studies, Science and Technical Subjects

Additional standards may be included and integrated into the activities in *Differentiated Activities and Assessments Using the Common Core Standards*. The following standards are those more observable in the activities within each topic.